THE NEW
SEAWEED
COOKBOOK

THE NEW
SEAWEED
COOKBOOK

A Complete Guide to Discovering
the Deep Flavors of the Sea

CRYSTAL JUNE MADERIA

Foreword by Josphine Spilka

North Atlantic Books
Berkeley, California

Published by North Atlantic Books
P.O. Box 12327
Berkeley, California 94712
Printed in the United States of America

Cover photos by Crystal Maderia
Cover and book design by
    Suzanne Albertson

The New Seaweed Cookbook is sponsored by the Society for the Study of Native Arts and Sciences, a nonprofit educational corporation whose goals are to develop an educational and cross-cultural perspective linking various scientific, social, and artistic fields; to nurture a holistic view of arts, sciences, humanities, and healing; and to publish and distribute literature on the relationship of mind, body, and nature.

North Atlantic Books' publications are available through most bookstores. For further information, visit our website at www.northatlanticbooks.com or call 800-733-3000.

Library of Congress Cataloging-in-Publication Data

Maderia, Crystal.
    The new seaweed cookbook : a complete guide to discovering the deep flavors of the sea / Crystal Maderia.
        p. cm.
    Includes index.
    ISBN 978-1-55643-652-9 (pbk.)
    1. Marine algae as food. 2. Cookery (Marine algae) I. Title.
    TX402.M324 2007
    641.6—dc22   2007012672

2 3 4 5 6 7 8 UNITED 18 17 16 15 14

TABLE OF CONTENTS

FOREWORD

by Josephine Spilka, Licensed Acupuncturist

Eating is a way of life. So ordinary and yet so potent, food is life itself. When we eat we know the world—the world common to all living things. It is quite possible to submerge such knowing in foods that dampen or dull our senses. Instead, here is a cookbook that can enliven and enrich your palate as well as your sensibilities. The recipes here invite you to become a part of the world, the actual world of eating, sensing, and knowing what it is to be alive, to enjoy life.

Seaweed, the focus of these recipes, is a nutrient-rich, often overlooked food that brings us to the ocean, the place where all life on this planet was conceived. The taste of seaweed brings the qualities of many worlds, both known and unknown. You have in this cookbook the advantages of an experienced food adventuress, whose insights and creations can take you to the depths, while keeping good company with the many practicalities of cooking.

In my work with health, I often remind people of the simple power of changing your diet. What you eat acts as medicine, as nourishment, as a political statement as well as the measure of nutrients consumed each day. Anything we must do over and over again gains momentum and strength—so, too, with our food. In opening our hearts and curiosity to where our food comes from and what energies it brings us, we can begin to harness that strength for our own growth and health. The most important change I ask people to make is to become conscious about what they are eating. To know the energy of what you eat, notice how you feel when you eat it. I do this by asking people to begin eating foods that require preparation, foods that start out fresh, unadulterated. In the process of choosing, handling, preparing, and eating foods we come to know so much more about who and what we are. I emphasize a diet of simple foods prepared in a myriad of ways, bright with color and texture. In this way, even though for many of us some foods are restricted, we can enjoy and celebrate our eating.

When I suggest to people that they change their diet, it is often in the presence of life-threatening illness, and the body has reached a point where it demands change. Still, it is often hard. We think the known will protect us, nourish us, and yet it is precisely the known habits that have brought us to where we are. Learning where our food comes from and how it is cultivated, we can start to loosen the habit of thinking that the unpackaged or unknown is unsafe, and begin to be excited by the world that demonstrates such infinite variety of flavor and color in our food.

Invoking both beauty and wonder, these recipes ease you into a great adventure—the adventure of coming to know one's body anew. Here in these pages through new foods and recipes you might awaken to the possibility that food can be a *gentle yet profound* medicine for changes you wish to see in your body and spirit. Know that by partaking of the individualized medicine of food choices, you bring about a larger healing, that of each person as they reconnect to the health of our world, both planet and people. Perhaps there is nothing one can say about food that is new in the world or that has not been articulated before, and yet for each of us discovering the power to know the world through our food choices is over and over again intoxicating.

DEDICATION AND
ACKNOWLEDGMENTS

In the nearly three-year process of writing this book, many times I have been comforted, supported, celebrated, and rescued by others. There were times (especially during editing) that I seriously questioned my intentions for this book, as well as my relationship to my work within this book. To all of those who believed in me, listened, encouraged, and nourished me during the process, I dedicate this book to our story as a family: my grandmother who eats seaweed every day and always tells me how much she loves it; my mother who filled our house with the smell of garlic and blueberry maple syrup cake; my father who read all of my prose through high school and gave me confidence in my writing; my sister who tries my recipes even when she doesn't want to; Helen in Motueka who cooked with me and for me, and with whom I have always shared a passion for food; Esme, Lindsay, Kate, Stephi, Krista, Johnny, and Raina, I cannot thank you all enough for listening to my endless hours of processing, offering childcare, and pushing me along the way to truly believe in myself; to my business partner and friend, Alanna, for your patience during the convergence of this book and our business plan; to the women of the moon circle for your support, confidence, and wisdom; to Deedee and Michelle for taking time out during your own independent and equally intense transitions to devote hours to editing my manuscript and helping me whip things into shape; to Aaron for your pep talk—your words helped me to stay focused; to Josephine, whose agreement to write the foreword for this book remains one of the biggest compliments I have ever received; to Denise whose ears have held my ramblings on more than a few occasions (Denise, you have loved me and supported me, and I am so thankful); to my children for teaching me about transition, helping me appreciate transformation, food, sensation, and sensitivity; and to my partner, who is the hardest-working person I know. Thank you for growing with me, loving me, supporting me through and through, and for being proud of me even when success feels distant.

There are many many people who have helped this book into being, some whose names I do not even know. To all of the sea vegetable harvesters and farmers, thank you for your stories, photos, and recipes. Thanks also to Richard Grossinger for picking my manuscript out of a pile, reading it through, and deciding to publish my book.

INTRODUCTION

Where I Come From

Throughout my whole life, food has been an essential element. When I was a child in Vermont, the seasons were marked with seasonal foods. Berries, cucumber salads, fresh herbs, autumn pumpkins, and apple feasts were enjoyed fresh during the summer and fall. In the winter I watched roots, venison, and turkey roasting in our wood stove that both heated our home and cooked our meals. Drops of fresh maple syrup came in the earliest bits of spring to mark the sweetness of summer that lay ahead; soon asparagus, wild leeks, and rhubarb would begin pushing their way through the newly thawed soil. Wild strawberries, concord grapes, golden apples, green beans, and blackberries drew me outdoors, stained my clothes, and gave me sustenance as my family's kitchen and garden offered me space to explore cultivation and food preparation.

When, in my early adolescence, my family courageously ventured to Mississippi, I found myself consoled and inspired by food and drawn to black-eyed peas, crayfish, collard greens, fried chicken, catfish, cornbread, and fresh warm honey. Like the air, the food was slow and thick, and different than anything I had tasted before. Pulled to discover the world through food, I sought cuisines and meals cooked with traditions from around the globe: Indian curries, sweet and spicy kofta, piles of papadoms, and pooris with chutneys and mint raita. Korean barbecues, Brazilian braises, Malaysian skewered meats. My entire history is a menu, and it is impossible for me to imagine it being any other way.

When I became a mother, my relationship with food offered me new opportunities for growth and education. My transition into motherhood was marked with my overwhelming need to nurture myself in ways I had never been responsible for before. My son was unsettled and required unusually high maintenance, so I changed my diet numerous times in an effort to comfort us. In the process, I discovered that my son suffered from sensitivities that could be mitigated by avoiding glutinous grains, dairy, nightshades, and corn. The impact of a restricted diet continues to affect me and has given me insight into diet and nutrition as well as enforced an intimate relationship with my family's health.

However, I have often doubted my fascination with food, criticizing myself for being so indulgent, or for putting so much energy into something so temporary; embarrassed that I wasted so much time sourcing a particular type of basil, or trying to make vegan marshmallows. Yet every day I am joyfully energized by this work. Transforming simple ingredients, eagerly awaiting the ripening of local fruit, and truly knowing what season it is by what is on my table helps me to feel connected to my life and to my community, and feeds me and my family in more ways than one.

In my work as a cook, caterer, and consultant to people with diet-specific needs, many people have asked me what to eat. I have tried numerous different products over time but am constantly humbled by the simple nourishment acquired through fresh, minimally processed, and wild foods. Like so many people that I have met, I consider wild foods such as sea vegetables to be an essential part of a healing diet, and yet there remains very little information in the Western world about how to purchase or prepare them. I now believe that instead of new products, people with diet-specific needs simply require more awareness and information on how to acquire and prepare the indigenous foods abundantly available.

My intention in writing this book is to make it possible for more people to have this information. In times of transition or celebration alike, I often look to the first food adventures for insight on how to re-connect with the basic art of cooking and sharing food. Roasting bones, gathering wild greens and sea vegetables, collecting seeds, and building fires—these acts ground me, pulling me into my alive-ness, and reminding me to appreciate my place in the food chain. Join me in this exploration, because great meals have a story, and I am constantly hungry for more.

About This Book

This book was born one afternoon on the coast of Mendocino, California. I was sitting with friends including Andrew and Tatiana of Pacific Wildcraft, munching sea palm fronds and talking about food. When someone commented that they loved the sea palm as a snack but didn't know how else to prepare it, Andrew and Tatiana noted that many of their customers shared this same dilemma. I sat quietly as Tatiana and Andrew discussed the marketing difficulties they face in selling their wild-harvested sea vegetables. Andrew and Tatiana are like many of the small food producers I have met; they do what they do because they love it and are motivated by their relationship to the process rather than by financial fantasies. They are committed to sustainable practices and yet, to maintain economic viability, they are having to constantly navigate through a predominantly mainstream market.

Like many other times when I heard people speak about food, I sat knowing that I had resources that could help—recipes and research collected over years. I told Tatiana and Andrew that I would like to put together a few recipes for them to offer their customers, and left the beach feeling excited and inspired by this food-related project that could potentially help a great number of people. Once I began going through my notes, however, I realized that I had an abundance of recipes and could perhaps write the first ever sea vegetable cookbook dedicated to total nourishment.

It seems that most people consider sea vegetables an essential part of a healthful diet, and yet there are really few resources that educate consumers on how to prepare them in alliance with other aspects of a healing diet or lifestyle. Sea vegetables are known to offer a great many health benefits and are quite possibly one of the most perfect foods for those observing special or restrictive diets. Despite these facts, inspiration is perhaps the most effective medicine. These recipes and the information in this book are to be used together to inspire even the most restrictive diet through a holistic approach.

In this book I will encourage you again and again to source your food directly. Whether you observe a specific diet or not, it is essential to know where your food comes from. Fresh food simply tastes better. Take the time to seek out the best-tasting, naturally raised and ripened foods, because the more energy you put into yourself through food, exercise, and/or education, the more energy you will have for yourself later. Use the directory in the back of this book to locate farmers in your region and to source essential pantry items like sea vegetables, salt, pepper, and coconut oil, enabling you to visualize yourself within, nurtured by the fabulous food chain.

About the Recipes

The great distances food often travels and the politics affecting the global food supply are issues that spark heated and unwinnable debates. What makes food "healthy" or one diet better than another? Such questions are on the minds of many that I have dined with, and the search for answers has motivated some people to adapt their diets in response to new information regarding politics, the environment, or health. For some, diet adaptations involve attempts to eat more nutrient-dense foods like sea vegetables; to stop or start eating meat, grow their own food, or use more organic ingredients; while for others diet changes may require a more complicated endeavor that involves the diagnosis of food sensitivities and elimination of certain foods.

As doctors become more aware of symptoms relating to food sensitivities, the group of diet-specific consumers has grown considerably. New products catering to gluten-, wheat-, and dairy-free diets are available in some places, but they tend to rely on heavily processed ingredients. Food sensitivities to nightshades, soy, or corn (for example) add further restrictions and are also difficult to avoid in most menus or recipes.

For those who want to dedicate themselves to their diet-specific needs as well as support sustainable food systems like organic agriculture and local food businesses, the act of collecting and cooking food can become overwhelmingly charged with anxiety, disappointment, and frustration. Friends, family, or even strangers joining together to share food can seem such a simple act, yet for those who have diet-specific needs, food may represent complex issues that make sharing a meal difficult to enjoy. Despite this dilemma, I have seen many people awaken with joy and inspiration by allowing themselves to create new connections with food through gardening, wild harvesting, experimenting with flavors, or simply learning about ingredients.

I often recommend sea vegetables to people who observe a special diet or are entering a diet transition. The unique flavors of sea vegetables awaken taste buds and complement a wide array of foods while providing concentrated nutritional value. The rich, dark green, purple, and black colors of sea vegetables always accentuate other colors on a plate and bring new awareness to everyday ingredients. Sea vegetables grow rapidly and are strong and durable while remaining flexible and flowing (in a word, resilient): perfect elements for those in a health transition. In addition, sea vegetables offer a diverse range of minerals essential to achieving and maintaining optimal health. B-vitamin folate, magnesium, iron, calcium, riboflavin, pantothenic acid, iodine, and lignans provide nourishment to the hormonal, lymphatic, urinary, circulatory, and nervous systems while soothing the digestive tract, dissolving fatty build-ups in the body, and protecting cells from cancer and radiation.

These sea vegetable recipes have been formulated to complement healing diets including those suggested for arthritis, autism, fibromyalgia, celiac disease, and dairy and wheat intolerances. The recipes in this book do not include ingredients commonly identified with sensitivities, intolerances, or allergies, such as:

cane sugar
cashews
canola oil
corn

glutinous grains:
  barley
  wheat
  rye
  spelt
  teff
  oats
milk products
peanuts
nightshades:
  eggplant (aubergine)
  potatoes, *not sweet potatoes*
  sweet and hot peppers (capsicum)
  tomatoes

Rather than fearing the restrictions of a chosen diet, allow limitations to become new boundaries in which to flourish. Discover the deep flavors of wild foods, committing a portion of your daily routine to celebrating the abundance of healthful ingredients. Share meals with intention and awareness, enjoying that which keeps us all alive and connected. Slow down to notice the days; each gives way to another, and seasons arrive filled with surprising new flavors, scents, and colors.

one

Sea Vegetables

Sea Vegetable Harvesters

There are many sea vegetable harvesters throughout the world who do not advertise or operate large-scale businesses. In many seaside villages, harvesters are individuals who collect sea vegetables for themselves and/or to sell at local markets. Along the coasts of Asia and Africa, larger operations are common as harvesters collect carrageen, nori, and kelp to sell to larger corporations, which then market the vegetables for a variety of uses from nori sheets to cosmetics to ice cream. I encourage you to establish a relationship with your food suppliers and, for the recipes in this book, to purchase high-quality sea vegetables directly from the harvesters or ask for them at your local natural food store. Here is a list of some of the harvesters whose sea vegetables I recommend. For contact information for these and other harvesters, see pages 140-142.

Pacific Wildcraft
Mendocino County, California
Andrew and Tatiana have been collecting sea vegetables from the Mendocino coast since the birth of their first child in 2000. Their family business has grown from their mutual love of working with the earth and the seasons, and the exhilaration they feel in their communication with the sea at low tide. Their work is a central aspect of their family, as Tatiana and Andrew dedicate themselves to the rhythm of nature, wild foods, and medicine. Pacific Wildcraft is a small family business that provides carefully selected wildfoods for healing, working with clients through direct and personal relationships. Pacific Wildcraft offers a variety of dried sea vegetables including sea palm, alaria, and nori.

Maine Coast Sea Vegetables
Franklin, Maine

Thirty-six years ago, Shep Erhart and his family began collecting sea vegetables for themselves on the northernmost shores of Maine. After a few years, they began marketing and developing their small sea vegetable business out of their home. Eventually, the operation moved from the family kitchen to the barn, then in the early Nineties to the present location. Maine Coast Sea Vegetables currently employs fifteen workers year round to process and package the range of sea vegetables harvested by more than forty harvesters on the "Down East" coast of Maine. The business is now governed by a group of four vested employees and Shep, collectively facing issues like livable wage, community outreach projects, benefits, healthcare, and company principles. When I asked Shep what he likes most about his business, he said, "I do what I do each day because I want to, because it feeds my heart, head and soul, because I see beauty in it everywhere, because this has been given to me to do today."

Quality Sea Veg
Cloughglass, County Donegal, Ireland

Quality Sea Veg is a certified organic sea vegetable company that collects and markets dulse, wakame, kombu, and carrageen. All of the sea vegetables are dried using fresh cool air, except the carrageen, which is dried in the sun and wind.

Ironbound Island Seaweed
Winter Harbor, Maine

Ironbound Island Seaweed is a worker-owned company dedicated to the sustainable harvest of wild sea vegetables. Their season begins in the early spring, in the dark hours of the morning low tide. The harvest is focused and intense, with the harvesters often wading waist-deep into waves to collect kombu, wakame, kelp, and dulse. Their sea vegetables are dried in the sun; and on foggy days, a wood-heated timber-framed drying house assists in the process.

Seagreens
West Sussex, United Kingdom and Norway

Seagreens provides specific varieties of wild Arctic brown "wrack" sea vegetables that are sustainably harvested. The sea vegetables are then processed by an Anglo-Norwegian joint venture to Demeter and Soil Association standards for use in organic foods and farming. The company is based in West Sussex and was Britain's first organic farm-to-table sea vegetable producer. Their website discusses health issues from autism and detoxification to cancer and obesity, in the company's efforts to "feed the foundation of health."

Pacific Harvest
New Zealand

Louise and Douglas Faucet host and participate in a long list of events throughout New Zealand and Asia, and they were awarded the "Best Local Flavor" honor during the 2005 Auckland Food Show. Through their business, they hope to make sea vegetables an integral part of the Western diet, and to offer a range of attractive sea vegetable products that cater to the nutritional and culinary needs of health-conscious customers and gourmands alike.

About the Sea Vegetables

Sea vegetables are diverse in flavor, texture, and nutritional value. Some are best enjoyed fresh, while others are dried and ground or re-hydrated before use. Some are used as foods, others as medicine, some are minimally processed, others more heavily. For those who live on the ocean's shores, seaweed is part of the everyday landscape. However, few people are aware that sea vegetables are regularly used to thicken, sweeten, and stabilize other foods. Large amounts of sea vegetables are collected for use in supplements, medicines, and vitamins, as well as for agricultural uses like organic fertilizer. Our world is dependent on sea vegetables, highlighted by the fact that fossilized sea vegetables are used every day by millions of people in the form of petroleum.

Despite the historical use of sea vegetables throughout the world, most people associate these ingredients with Asian food such as sushi or "seaweed salad." Sea vegetables are frequently located in the Asian food section of grocery and natural food stores, or with other ethnic foods. Varieties are often limited to what is available through large distribution companies, so finding a particular type or brand of sea vegetable may be difficult. Check out what is available, and try several varieties to see which flavors or textures you are most attracted to. Often sea vegetable harvesters are happy to send small samples to get you started (see the Sources section in the back of this book). Dried sea vegetables store well in airtight containers, so you can keep several varieties on hand or order a larger quantity of a particular variety without worry of the sea vegetables going bad.

Looking to eat more sea vegetables? Listed below is a selection of sea vegetables that are easily found or purchased for culinary uses.

Agar

Agar is a product of extraction from a variety of red sea vegetables, used extensively as a vegetarian gelling agent.

Arame

An excellent sea vegetable to have on hand, arame reconstitutes quickly in warm water and is mild in flavor and texture. Arame is related to kelp. It is actually a large vegetable, cut into thin strips and dried for easier storage. Arame can be used alternatively with hijiki.

Alaria, or "Winged Kelp"

Sometimes labeled as wakame, alaria is similar in flavor, texture, and appearance but is a different species. It is sweet in flavor, and when reconstituted, rich in texture.

Bullwhip Kelp, also known as Seawhip

Rarely sold in stores, this variety of seaweed can be ordered directly from sea vegetable harvesters. This easily identified plant grows prolifically on most coasts. It is easy to harvest during low tide, and both the fronds and the thick hollow "stem" are full of nutrients and unique flavor.

Carrageen
Used for centuries in Ireland, carrageen is now a common ingredient in many packaged foods today. Traditionally carrageen is served in the form of a sweet milky pudding, and is incorporated with oats and pan-fried as a nurturing breakfast food. It is sweet and soft, and can replace agar in some recipes.

Dulse
Used extensively in native dishes throughout the UK, Norway, and eastern parts of North America, dulse has a very salty flavor, and when toasted it offers a crispness that quickly melts on your tongue. Look for the purple dulse packaged still slightly moist. Seek out smoked dulse too!

Hijiki
Mild in flavor yet deep black in color, this sea vegetable is a beautiful addition to many dishes from salads to roasted meats or vegetable stir-fries. Soak to reconstitute and watch it expand up to four times its dried size!

Karengo *(Porphyra)*
Dark green and slightly purplish, this thin, hand-sized vegetable is collected off shoreline rocks in cold waters. It has a mild flavor and can be prepared in numerous ways. Often karengo is used as a snack food as well as a condiment to grains and egg dishes. You can purchase karengo in flakes and powders as well as dried fronds.

Kombu/Kelp *(Laminaria)*
These strips should be dark black or green, although the texture and color does vary from season to season, depending on the age of the

plant. Kombu is the essential ingredient in dashi broth and can be used to enhance the flavor of almost any dish. Kombu and kelps contain sodium glutamate, often referred to as "natural MSG." I add a stick of kombu to beans to help bring flavor as well as to encourage digestibility. Kombu is harvested from late spring to early fall, making it an ideal ingredient for summer and fall meals.

Nori (Laver, *Porphyra*)
Collected throughout the coastal areas of the world, nori has provided nutrients and flavor to indigenous coastal communities for generations. Nori is abundant and easy to harvest, making it one of the most available sea vegetables on the market today. Nori is the sea vegetable used to make nori and sushi paper, but it is also available in less processed forms when bought directly from sea vegetable harvesters.

Ogo *(Gracilaria)*
A very popular sea vegetable in Hawaii, ogo is often used fresh in salads and pickles, and is a source of agar.

Sea Lettuce
Delicately thin and leaf-like, sea lettuce is used fresh or reconstituted for sea vegetable salad.

Sea Palm
Sea palm is sold as either fronds or blades. The fronds are the tender tips, or the younger parts of the plant, and the blades are the more mature, longer version. Both are excellent soaked and cooked with lemon. The tender fronds are sometimes sold dried and mixed with toasted almonds or pumpkin seeds, a great summer snack!

Wakame
This sea vegetable is popular throughout the world for its slightly sweet flavor and tender texture. It is traditionally used in Japan to make a sea vegetable salad or added to summer miso soup.

Tapping into the Deeper Well

Like the water is to the earth, the deeper well is a place within us all that knows exactly what we need. It is a place that helps us heal from wounds, illness, and trauma. It is our thermal mass, our regulator, our center. When new information tells us that we must change, it is the deeper well within that keeps us connected to our truth. It is our dearest asset and the source of our inspiration to grow. From the deeper well, we draw our courage to transform, to be in harmony, and to assimilate new information. Despite whatever hardships we meet or confusions we come across, when we tap into the deeper well, we are carried on a current towards our greater health.

two

Seasonings
and Dressings

Spices and Powders

Nori Nettle Gomasio

This is a beautiful condiment with a mix of black, white, and green. Gomasio is often used in place of salt to add calcium and extra fiber to prepared foods. Nettles are a wild green (also known as stinging nettles) rich in iron and flavor, harvested in spring, and dried to use throughout the year. To learn more about where these plants grow, their nutritional and healing qualities, or where to purchase them, contact your local herbalist or natural foods store.

> equal parts in weight:
> dried nettle tops
> nori
> hulled sesame seeds
> black sesame seeds

Combine all the ingredients and crush in mortar or spice grinder. Store in an airtight glass container.

Seven Spices Blend

Seaweed is a natural ingredient in this somewhat traditional Japanese spice mixture. This blend gives depth to steamed veggies and fried tofu, as well as broths and meat marinades.

> 1 cup loosely packed, toasted wild nori pieces
> 1 tablespoon poppy seeds
> 2 tablespoons prepared hemp or sesame seeds
> peels of 2 tangerines, dried
> 2 tablespoons Szechuan peppercorns *or* 2 teaspoons cayenne
>   and 1 tablespoon black peppercorns
> 1 tablespoon mustard seeds, soaked and toasted

Prepare the seeds and set aside to cool. Crumble nori sheets between your hands, then add all ingredients to a mortar or spice grinder. Grind until fine. Store in a shaker or airtight container.

Tangy Korean Nori

This is a great condiment and snack (serve sheets uncrushed) and only takes a few minutes to prepare.

> 12 sheets nori
> 1 tablespoon ginger juice
> 1 clove garlic
> 3 tablespoons Bragg Liquid Aminos *or* 1 tablespoon
>   umeboshi plum vinegar
> 2 tablespoons honey
> $1/2$ teaspoon cayenne

Preheat oven to 350°F.

Juice ginger and garlic in a vegetable juicer. Mix the garlic/ginger juice with the other liquid ingredients in a spray bottle (shake well). Warm the broiler in your toaster oven and arrange two sheets of nori on each cookie sheet. Spray each piece of nori then sprinkle on the cayenne. Toast two pieces at a time until crisp, remove from the oven, and cool. When cool, crumple between your hands, then grind in mortar or spice grinder. Store in an airtight container or shaker.

Zesty Peck

This seasoning has so many beautiful qualities: smoky, tangy, and savory. I like it most as a condiment to sauce-based dishes and as a seasoning for chicken. Like it sounds, it's zesty, like a peck on the cheek.

> $3/4$ cup fresh rosemary
> $3/4$ cup fresh sage
> 3 tablespoons fresh lemon thyme

2 heads crushed garlic (¼ cup)
¼ cup dried sea palm fronds
1 tablespoon crushed black peppercorns
3 tablespoons organic lemon zest
¼ cup smoked dulse

Combine fresh herbs and chop together to blend. Crush sea palm in a spice grinder and then add black peppercorns, lemon zest, and smoked dulse. Pulse until well crushed. Combine chopped herbs, crushed garlic, and sea vegetable mixture in a mortar and grind together with a pestle until well combined and crumb-like. Store this mixture in the refrigerator in an airtight container.

Spice of Amazigh

This condiment is adapted from a traditional North African meat rub. It is an aromatic seasoning that works equally well for meat or vegetables. Each individual spice offers digestive support, and together they offer a unique combination that is both warming and cooling.

⅛ cup dried mint (or 3 tablespoons fresh mint)
1 tablespoon black royal cumin
1 tablespoon coriander seeds
½ teaspoon cardamom seeds
1 teaspoon fenugreek seeds
½ teaspoon fresh shaved nutmeg
1 teaspoon fresh shaved cinnamon
1 teaspoon whole cloves
½ teaspoon allspice berries
1 tablespoon black peppercorns
3 tablespoons sea palm fronds
2 teaspoons ginger powder (or 2 tablespoons fresh ginger juice)

Toast all of the ingredients until fragrant, cool, then grind in a spice grinder or with a mortar and pestle.

Alternatively, this spice can be made with fresh herbs, resulting in a paste rather than a powder. Gather 1 cup of fresh mint, process until smooth, and add to the powdered spices. Store in the refrigerator.

Moroccan Spice Rub

This is an inspiring blend that lends itself to eclectic fusion-style cooking. This works well with tofu and tempeh as well as lamb, chicken, and pilafs, and is great added to dressings or marinades.

1 head of garlic
thumb-size piece of ginger
peel of 1 organic orange
peel of 1 organic lemon
¼ cup whole kelp
1 tablespoon whole coriander seeds
¼ cup fennel seeds
½ tablespoon whole cumin seeds
1 tablespoon pink peppercorns
2 teaspoons black peppercorns
2 tablespoons cinnamon
½ teaspoon cayenne

Preheat oven to 200°F.

Slice garlic, ginger, and citrus peels ultra thin with a mandolin or sharp knife. Put ginger, garlic, citrus peels, and kelp on baking sheets and place in the oven to dry for approximately 3 hours. Or dry in a dehydrator overnight. Kelp will dry quickly, and it can be removed after a few minutes and placed in an airtight container until other ingredients are ready. Toast coriander, fennel, and cumin in a hot skillet until fragrant and the fennel begins to look toasted. Once cool, combine all ingredients in a spice grinder and pulse until powdered.

Pumpkin Seed Crust

This is a handy mixture to have around for coating tofu, fish, or chicken. It can be used to replace bread crumbs or flour in pan-fried recipes, in addition to adding variety and texture to otherwise simple recipes.

> 1 cup prepared pumpkin seeds
> 1 cup dried sea palm

Prepare pumpkin seeds and pulse with dried sea palm in a spice grinder until crumb-like in texture. Store in an airtight container.

Seasoned Rice Flour

Making this flour is very satisfying. It is better than anything like it I've found in the store, and it is so simple and has so many uses, you'll have to try it. Be sure to keep plenty on hand. Store in the freezer or a glass airtight container on a cool shelf.

> 1 cup sushi rice
> 1½ cups arrowroot
> 1 cup organic brown rice cream hot cereal (uncooked)
> ⅛ cup kelp powder
> 2 tablespoons crushed green peppercorns
> 1 tablespoon crushed Szechuan peppercorns

Pulse the sushi rice in a spice grinder until very fine, combine all ingredients, and store.

Pink Table Salts

When you want to bring awareness into each detail of your meal, pay particular attention to texture and color. Dulse adds color and minerals to unrefined salts, and this is a great way to bring attention to an often-overlooked ingredient.

> 1 cup unrefined solar-dried sea salt, Himalayan salt crystals,
>   or Utah solar-dried mineral salt
> ½ cup dulse pieces

Be sure that the dulse is dry (if not, gently toast in oven or cast-iron skillet on medium heat), then finely crush in a mortar or with a spice grinder. Mix the dulse and the salt together and store in a salt shaker.

Kombu Shiitake Shake

This powder can be used in miso soup, vegan onion soup, simple broths, or as a coating for fried tofu or fish. It is rich and deep, offering flavor from the earth and the sea.

> 3 cups dried shiitake mushrooms
> 3 sticks dried kombu

Pulse together in a spice grinder and store in an airtight container.

Dressings and Condiments

Nori Marinade with Lime

Subtle and unusual, this condiment lends an exotic element to chicken, shellfish, and roasted roots.

> ¼ cup dry nori
> ½ cup fresh tarragon leaves and tips
> ⅔ cup fresh lime juice
> ½ cup kombu stock

Pulse nori in a spice grinder. Process the tarragon in a mortar or a blender until nearly puréed. Combine all ingredients and blend again with a whisk or blender.

Dark Gingered Marinade

Deep, dark, and daring. This recipe is great as a quick marinade for summer grilling or pan searing.

> ½ cup chopped scallions
> ½ cup toasted crushed nori

1 cup dashi (see page 125)
3 tablespoons ginger juice
2 cloves minced garlic
½ teaspoon soaked Asian mustard seeds
wheat-free tamari or Bragg Liquid Aminos to taste

Put all ingredients in a blender and blend until well combined.

Sea Palm Salad Dressing

This recipe is worth getting to know. Use it as is or as a base for other flavors. Excellent as a dressing as well as a marinade. Beautiful on salmon, chicken, tofu, roasted veggies, and grains.

1 tablespoon grated lemon peel
1 tablespoon soaked yellow mustard seeds
1 cup fresh lemon juice
½ cup minced shallots
1 cup dry sea palm
1 tablespoon maple syrup (optional)
dashi as needed
Bragg Liquid Aminos to taste

Crush lemon peel and mustard seeds together. Put all ingredients in a blender and let soak until liquid is absorbed considerably. Blend, adding dashi stock as needed to adjust consistency. (Dashi recipe on page 125.)

Vanilla Kombu Aioli with Lime Cumin Variation, and Green Peppercorn Cream Option

These three aiolis are tangy, creamy, and smooth. They can be thinned with water or vegan yogurt (my favorite is Wildwood Soy brand) or an unsweetened non-dairy milk and additional lemon juice.

1 cup pine nuts *or* 1 cup soft silken tofu
1 stick kombu

½ Tahitian vanilla pod, split down the middle
3 cups water
⅓ cup fresh Meyer lemon juice
1 tablespoon olive oil

Soak pine nuts in 1 cup of water for 3 hours. Soak kombu in the remaining 2 cups of water for 1 hour (it will swell), then combine with the vanilla pod and simmer on medium until liquid is reduced to half a cup. Cool and strain. In a blender, purée pine nuts (or tofu if using) with kombu, vanilla, and liquid, as well as half of the lemon juice. Add lemon juice and olive oil to taste. If the aioli is not smooth even after blending, strain through a cheesecloth or clean tea towel and store in the refrigerator.

Lime Cumin Aioli (variation)

1 cup pine nuts *or* 1 cup soft silken tofu
1 stick kombu
3 cups water
¼ cup lemon juice
⅛ cup lime juice
1 tablespoon cumin seeds, toasted and ground
1 tablespoon olive oil

Soak pine nuts in 1 cup of the water for 3 hours; drain. On medium heat, simmer kombu in remaining water until liquid is reduced to half a cup. Purée pine nuts (or tofu if using) with kombu and simmering liquid, as well as half of the lemon juice and all of the lime juice. Add the cumin and adjust taste with more lemon juice and olive oil.

Green Peppercorn Cream Aioli

1 cup pine nuts *or* 1 cup soft silken tofu
1 stick kombu
3 cups water
1 tablespoon green peppercorns
⅓ cup organic lemon juice
1 tablespoon olive oil

Soak pine nuts in 1 cup of water for 3 hours; drain. Soak kombu for 1 hour in 2 cups of water, then simmer on medium until the liquid is reduced to a half a cup. Use a spice grinder to powder the green peppercorns.

In a blender, purée pine nuts (or tofu if using), kombu and simmering liquid, half of the lemon juice, and the peppercorn powder. Adjust to taste with olive oil and remaining lemon juice.

Pink Kombu Mustard Sauce

Pink peppercorns are not actually related to either black peppers or capsicums, but are in the rose family. The floral aroma and herbal sweetness stimulate the senses and complement cold meats and roasted vegetables nicely.

> ½ cup dashi (see page 125)
> ½ stick kombu reserved from basic dashi recipe
> ½ cup apple cider vinegar
> ¼ cup pink peppercorns
> ½ cup mustard seeds (yellow or brown)
> 1 tablespoon dried red raspberries or 1/4 cup strained
>   raspberry juice
> 1 tablespoon raw honey (optional)

Combine all ingredients except the honey and soak for at least 24 hours and up to 48 hours, adding more dashi as needed to keep the seeds covered. In a small food processor, pulse all of the ingredients until peppercorns have been crushed and mustard is creamy. Sweeten with honey to taste (optional).

Seaweed and Sauerkraut

Pickled vegetables are an essential part of most indigenous cuisines. They stimulate digestion, add essential flavors to a menu, and provide beneficial bacteria. I offer below three recipes for fermented vegetables that include sea vegetables. I encourage you to add pickled condiments to your menu and experience the benefits yourself. This first one is a recipe from *Healing with Whole Foods* by Paul Pitchford (North Atlantic Books).

Crystal Maderia

Seaweed and Sauerkraut

> 1 head cabbage, sliced thin, outer leaves saved
> ½ cup dulse, torn and soaked

Mix sliced cabbage with dulse. In a large wooden bowl, pound cabbage and dulse with a wooden mallet to release juices. Put cabbage-dulse mixture in a glass container or a ceramic pot and cover with reserved outer leaves of cabbage. Rest a clean plate directly on the cabbage. Place a weight on the plate to compress the mixture, and cover the whole container with a large piece of cheesecloth, then a loose-fitting lid. Set aside in a cool place. After one week the contents should be fermenting. The cabbage should be submerged in brine and contents should not have mold. Remove outer leaves and store in glass containers in refrigerator.

Korean Kimchee with Sea Veggies

When people insist that they don't like sauerkraut, I recommend kimchee. The spicy sour notes complement tempeh and go well with anything barbecued.

> 1 head green cabbage, sliced, outer leaves saved
> 3 long daikon radishes in silver-dollar slices

2 cups grated carrots

½ cup grated ginger

1 cup arame

1 teaspoon cayenne pepper *or* 1 fresh cayenne pepper, seeds
removed, thinly sliced

3 cups water

Soak cabbage, daikon, and carrots overnight in water. Strain and combine with the rest of the ingredients. Proceed according to the Seaweed and Sauerkraut recipe above.

Pickled Bullwhip

Bullwhip pickles are a treat worth having on hand. Like most good pickles, these are sweet, salty, sour, and slightly spicy. They go really well with the Vegan "Tuna" Salad (page 48) and are ideal in any picnic basket.

2 cups apple cider vinegar

1 cup apple cider

½ cup finely grated fresh horseradish

1 small dried chile

1 tablespoon yellow mustard seeds

2 cloves garlic, sliced

1½ cups dried sliced bullwhip *or* 3 cups fresh bullwhip, sliced

1 teaspoon salt

2 tablespoons honey

Combine all ingredients and cover with a clean plate and a weight that keeps the bullwhip below the liquid. Cover the container with cheesecloth and a loose lid and leave in a cool place for 2 or 3 days. Check every day, and if using dry bullwhip, add vinegar to keep the sea vegetables submerged. Taste before transferring to smaller containers. Add salt and honey according to taste.

Gorgeous Fennel Palm Dressing

This is an ideal marinade for late-summer vegetables, especially those you plan to broil, roast, or grill. It also makes a beautiful dressing for quinoa or warm grain salads. The lightness of this recipe is reminiscent of summer and the foods of that season.

2 tablespoons fennel seeds
½ cup fennel fronds
¼ cup water
½ teaspoon orange rind
1 teaspoon turmeric
1 teaspoon mirin *or* ½ teaspoon rice vinegar and 1 teaspoon honey
½ teaspoon sesame oil
1 tablespoon sea palm

Toast fennel seeds in a hot skillet until they are fragrant. Grind in a spice grinder or with a mortar and pestle. Combine the rest of the ingredients except sea palm in a blender and purée until smooth. Strain this liquid, pushing all of the oil and juices through the strainer. Crush the sea palm and add to the liquid.

Smoky Cajun Oil

Bearing qualities of a jerk marinade, this condiment is spicy, sweet, salty, and tangy with a smoky undertone. Use this oil as an accent seasoning (drizzled on after food has been cooked), as well as a marinade for tofu, tempeh, lamb, mushrooms, chicken, and shellfish.

½ cup dates
½ ounce smoked or regular dulse
1 tablespoon black peppercorns
½ teaspoon dried ground coriander
¼ teaspoon ground caraway
1 teaspoon Atlantic smoked salt
1 tablespoon paprika (optional)
1 bay leaf

1 tablespoon salt
1/2 teaspoon black pepper
1/2 cup apple cider
3 tablespoons lemon juice
2 cloves garlic
1/2 cup fresh coriander
2 tablespoons fresh lemon thyme
1 cup olive oil

Soak dates in water to cover for 1 hour (up to overnight). Toast dulse in a warm oven until crisp, about 10 minutes at 300°F. Cool. Toast seeds and various peppercorns in a hot skillet until fragrant then grind with dulse until powdered. Combine powders. Combine dates (save liquid), apple cider, lemon juice, garlic, fresh coriander, and lemon thyme in a food processor or with an immersion blender and pulse until smooth. Add olive oil if it seems dry. Add in the rest of the olive oil at the end and slowly add the fine powder. Add date liquid to taste. Store in the refrigerator for up to 2 weeks.

Cranberry Sauce

Cranberries are an ingredient we see a lot around the autumn and winter holidays. This is when they are in season and when we need the cheerful red color in our diet as well as the sour flavors to tease our taste buds.

2 1/2 tablespoons agar flakes
2 1/2 cups apple cider
1 orange, tangerine, or mandarin, seeds removed, cut into thin slices
3 cups cranberries

Combine agar and apple cider and soak 15 minutes. Bring to a slow boil for approximately 15 minutes while stirring. Add orange slices and cranberries; return to boiling. Lower heat and cook on low for about 15 minutes, stirring and mashing the cranberries and oranges. Pour into a mold or a bowl and let cool. Cover and refrigerate.

three

Small Dishes, Appetizers, and Salads

Sea Palm Straight Up

Sea palm grows wild on the northern coast of California and is a popular snack and health food for many who live there. This dish is a straightforward recipe that showcases the subtle sweetness and sensual tenderness of the sea palm, as well as complements many other foods from the northern California region.

> 4 cups sea palm
> enough water to cover
> 1 lemon, seeds removed
> 2 tablespoons heating oil (see discussion of heating oil
>   in back of book)
> 2 tablespoons olive oil

Let the sea palm soak for about half an hour or until it has absorbed some of the water and is limp. Drain, and reserve soaking water. Cut half of the lemon into very thin slices.

Heat a large skillet and sauté the sea palm and lemon slices on high heat, adding bits of the soaking water when the pan seems dry. Test the sea palm after 10 minutes.

Place the sea palm in a bowl and season with olive oil and lemon juice.

Crystal Maderia

Sea Palm Straight Up

Sautéed Wakame with Green Beans

Wakame and green beans complement each other here, and give life to the spring or summer table. Bring this dish along to your next summer barbecue or potluck and watch as everyone devours it!

4 cups dried wakame, soaking
1 pound green beans
1 tablespoon heating oil
1 teaspoon wheat-free tamari or Bragg Liquid Aminos
2 tablespoons prepared sesame seeds

Soak the wakame in enough water to cover. When the wakame is soft, remove from the water and slice into long thin strips, discarding the center rib.

Trim the green beans and place in a large pot of boiling water for 2 minutes. Drain and run under cold water until cool to retain crispness and color.

Heat a large cast-iron skillet on medium-high heat. Sauté the green beans for 3 minutes. Add the heating oil and wakame. Continue to sauté for 3–4 minutes. Remove from heat and toss with tamari and sesame seeds. Serve hot or cold.

Basic Arame Slaw

Arame salad has been a traditional side dish in the health food and vegetarian restaurant industries for years. Many restaurants have their own version of this recipe. This version is simple and easy to make. Arame is tender, mild, and slightly sweet, and therefore popular with many who otherwise find sea vegetables too overwhelming.

2 cups dried arame
1½ cups water
¼ cup mirin
½ tablespoon umeboshi plum vinegar
1 cup purple cabbage, shredded

$\frac{1}{2}$ cup carrots, shredded
$\frac{1}{2}$ cup gold beet, shredded
1 teaspoon grated ginger
$\frac{1}{4}$ cup flat parsley, minced
1 tablespoon lemon juice
1 tablespoon prepared sesame seeds
cayenne to taste

Soak the arame in water for 30 minutes. Drain. In a large bowl, mix the remaining ingredients. Add the arame and season with cayenne to taste.

Hijiki Caviar on Rice Crisps with Lemon Tahini

This is an elegant appetizer to surprise guests with on a special occasion. Prepare the caviar and tahini sauce ahead of time, then top the rice crackers just before serving.

"caviar"
1 cup dried hijiki
$\frac{3}{4}$ cup water
a dash of mirin
2 tablespoons wheat-free tamari *or* $\frac{1}{2}$ tablespoon
    umeboshi plum paste
$\frac{1}{8}$ cup onion, minced (optional)
1 teaspoon ginger juice
1 tablespoon lemon juice
1 teaspoon sea salt
1 teaspoon sesame oil
tahini sauce
1 cup sesame tahini
$\frac{1}{2}$ cup water
$\frac{1}{2}$ cup lemon juice
$\frac{1}{2}$ tablespoon garlic juice
1 tablespoon wheat-free tamari *or* salt to taste

2 dozen brown rice crackers (see Sources)

Hijiki Caviar on Rice Crisps with Lemon Tahini

Soak the hijiki for 5 minutes in cold water. Drain. In a medium skillet, heat the ¾ cup water, mirin, and tamari. Add the hijiki and simmer on medium heat for 5 minutes. Add the onion (if using) and ginger juice and continue to cook uncovered until all of the liquid has evaporated. Remove from heat; add the lemon juice, salt, and sesame oil. Set aside to cool completely.

To make the lemon tahini sauce, combine all the tahini, water, lemon, and garlic juice and season with tamari or salt. Add water until the sauce is smooth and runs freely off the edge of a spoon.

To serve, place the crackers in a straight line on waxed paper. Starting at one end of the line, drizzle the tahini sauce over the bottom half of each cracker. Drop one spoonful of the hijiki on top of the tahini, and arrange the crackers on a serving tray with additional lemon wedges.

Baked Stuffed Shiitake

Shiitake mushrooms have a unique woodsy aroma and meaty flavor that goes well with the subtly wild and sweet flavors of arame. These stuffed shiitake are an elegant menu item for which it is worthwhile to source the best ingredients. Sources for mushroom kits and mushroom harvesters are listed on page 139.

1 cup dried arame

1 cup water

¼ cup mirin

2 tablespoons lemon juice

2 tablespoons wheat-free tamari or Bragg Liquid Aminos

¼ cup onion, minced

1 clove garlic, minced

½ teaspoon ginger juice

2 large shiitake mushrooms, stems removed

6 scallions, finely chopped

1 tablespoon sesame oil

2 tablespoons plum sauce (optional—see page 65)

Soak the arame for 10 minutes. Drain. Cook the arame with 1 cup water on high heat for 10 minutes. Drain. Mix together the mirin, lemon juice, tamari, onion, and ginger juice; divide into two portions and set aside.

In a medium skillet, sauté the arame with half of the mirin mixture. Cook on medium-high heat for 5 minutes, or until all of the liquid is absorbed. Remove from heat.

Preheat the oven to 350°F.

Place the shiitakes in the bottom of a large glass baking dish. Mound the arame mixture on top of each mushroom. Pour the remaining half of the mirin mixture around the mushrooms. Bake in the oven for 15–20 minutes.

Remove from heat and drizzle with the scallions, sesame oil, and plum sauce. Serve hot.

Mock Calamari with Seawhip Tartar

Let's face it, this recipe is built on lies! Mock calamari? Seaweed tartar sauce?

This tasty snack is best piled high on a plate and served right away.

2 cups dried whole nori (not nori sheets)
½ teaspoon baking powder
2 cups arrowroot powder
½ cup white rice flour
2 tablespoons peppercorns, ground
1 teaspoon dried turmeric
1 teaspoon fine salt
heating oil

1 cup Green Peppercorn Cream Aioli (see pages 26-27)
¼ cup Pickled Bullwhip, minced (see page 29)
1 clove garlic, minced

coarse sea salt

To make the nori tempura a.k.a. "mock calamari":

First soak nori in cool water for 15 minutes, or until soft and pliable. Drain and tear roughly into 2-inch pieces. Combine baking powder and arrowroot and rice flours with ground pepper, turmeric, and salt. Combine nori and the flour mixture, and toss until well coated.

In a large cast-iron skillet, heat the heating oil on medium-high. When melted, the oil should fill the bottom inch of the pan. When a small bit of batter dropped into the oil sizzles and bubbles quickly, the oil is ready. Fry the nori in batches, maintaining the oil temperature so the sea vegetables don't burn.

The nori is done when it is golden brown and crisp on the outside. Drain nori on a muslin-lined baking sheet. Sprinkle with coarse sea salt before serving.

To make the tartar sauce:

Mix the aioli, pickled bullwhip, and the garlic, and set aside.

Serve the nori hot with the seawhip tartar and extra lemon wedges.

Oyster Mushroom and Artichoke Custard with Steamed Antipasto Veggies and Mochi Crudités

This recipe consists of several parts. Individually they are each satisfying; together they are a complete symphony of texture and flavor.

oyster mushroom and artichoke custard
- 1½ cups oyster mushrooms, washed and chopped
- 1½ cups artichoke hearts, hairs removed, minced
- 2–6 cloves garlic, peeled
- 2 cups Green Peppercorn Cream Aioli *or* 2 cups silken tofu blended with 3 tablespoons lemon juice and salt to taste
- ¼ cup dried sea palm fronds, broken into small pieces
- 1 tablespoon ground flax seeds
- 2 cloves garlic, minced (optional)

steamed antipasto veggies
- ½ pound baby carrots with green tops
- ½ pound baby beets
- ½ pound early green beans
- ¼ pound baby turnips with green tops

mochi crudités
- 1 package seeded mochi, grated
- 3 tablespoons arame or hijiki, soaked, drained and minced
- 2 tablespoons Atlantic smoked salt *or* crushed smoked dulse
- 1 tablespoon lemon juice
- 2 tablespoons heating oil

To make the custard:

Preheat oven to 350°F. Have ready a medium-sized baking dish.

Combine all of the custard ingredients and pour into the baking dish. Bake uncovered for 45 minutes, or until bubbly and cooked through. Remove from the oven, cover, and let the custard rest for at least 10 minutes.

While the custard is baking, wash and trim all of the veggies, leaving just the very bottom of the greens intact on the root vegetables. Place turnips and beets in a steaming tray above a large pot of boiling water. Steam for 5 minutes. Add carrots; steam for an additional 10 minutes. Add green beans and steam another 5 minutes, or until green beans are tender. Plunge all of the vegetables into ice water, and drain. Toss with coarse salt (or dulse), and set aside.

To make the crudités:

Preheat oven to 425°F. Mix together all of the crudité ingredients except the heating oil. Oil a large baking sheet, and place tablespoons of the mochi mixture onto the sheet. Place in the oven. Bake for 5–10 minutes, watching closely so as not to burn, and remove from the oven when the mochi has melted and is crisp.

Serve the custard alongside the steamed veggies and mochi crudités.

Beef Mango Spring Rolls

Salads and fruits don't have to be boring when you use leftover grilled beef, as in this recipe. In fact, make extra on purpose, so that you can throw together some spring rolls for a quick lunch on a hot summer day.

filling

1–2 cups seared beef, shredded
1 large mango, minced
$\frac{1}{2}$ cup fresh baby mint or mint leaves, chopped
$\frac{1}{4}$ cup fresh cilantro
$\frac{1}{2}$ cup soaked arame, chopped
$\frac{1}{2}$ cup carrots, shredded
$\frac{1}{2}$ cup radishes, shredded
$\frac{1}{2}$ cup grated cucumber
3 tablespoons lemon juice
1 tablespoon lime juice
1 tablespoon mirin
$\frac{1}{4}$ cup Dark Gingered Marinade (see page 24)

2 cups cooked white rice noodles, cooled
1 head of washed lettuce leaves, drained
large rice paper wrappers

In a large bowl, mix together the ingredients for the filling. Let rest for about 10 minutes while you prepare your work station.

Have ready rice paper wrappers, a clean work surface, and a large bowl of cold water to soften the wrappers. Also have ready rice noodles and lettuce leaves.

To roll spring rolls, first soften a wrapper by dipping into cool water, removing from water as soon as the wrapper is pliable. Shake off excess water.

Place the softened wrapper on top of your work surface.

Place several lettuce leaves off center on the wrapper. Top with a few spoonfuls of the beef mango mixture, and then several strands of rice noodles. Wrap the rice paper around the filling tightly, careful not to tear. If the wrapper is too wet it will be more difficult. The wrapper should be stretchy and sticky. As you work with them you will discover your technique, so if one falls apart, just move on to the next. Practice rolling with the same mixture until you feel confident to continue with the rest of your ingredients.

Sweet Potato Pom Poms

This is another child-friendly food. Here, sweet potatoes are formed into balls with sea vegetables, quickly fried, and decorated with a coating of sea vegetable flakes. If you have helping fingers in the kitchen, use them here!

3 sweet potatoes, boiled, mashed, and cooled
½ cup dried hijiki, soaked, drained, and minced
1 cup seasoned rice flour (see page 23) *or* (for less spice)
    white rice flour
1 teaspoon grated ginger
1 tablespoon wheat-free tamari *or* 1 teaspoon
    umeboshi plum paste

heating oil

½ cup Tangy Korean Nori powder (see page 20)

Preheat oven to 350°F. Mix sweet potatoes with hijiki, rice flour, ginger, and tamari. Form into walnut-sized balls and set aside.

Melt the heating oil in a cast-iron skillet. When the oil is shimmering, fry the balls until golden and crisp.

Roll the balls in the crushed nori and place on a baking sheet lined with parchment paper. Bake for 5 minutes, or until the nori is crisp.

African Meat Samosas with Pomegranate Dipping Sauce and Nori Lime Dressing

Wheat- and gluten-free samosas! These store well in the freezer and can be reheated in the oven without a problem. This recipe is versatile and can be made with the equivalent amount of chickpeas, ground turkey, or ground beef.

filling

2 pounds ground lamb, turkey, chickpeas, or beef

¼ cup Spice of Amazigh (see page 21)

1 small onion, minced

1 cup cooked lentils (green or red)

2 tablespoons wheat-free tamari

pastry

1½ cups millet flour

2 cups arrowroot or tapioca flour

1½ cups brown rice flour

1 cup white rice flour

2 teaspoons fine salt

2 eggs, beaten, or egg substitution

1½ cups heating oil, melted

2½ cups cold water, as needed

2 tablespoons cumin seeds, toasted and ground

1 tablespoon black pepper, coarsely ground

$\frac{1}{2}$ tablespoon white pepper, ground

3 tablespoons heating oil

pomegranate sauce

1$\frac{1}{2}$ cups pomegranate juice

1 cup Nori Marinade with Lime dressing (see page 24)

Mix the lamb with spices, onion, lentils, and tamari and refrigerate overnight.

Combine flours for the pastry and stir in salt, eggs, oil, and enough water to make into a dough. When all of the flour has been mixed in, incorporate pepper and cumin and beat with a wooden spoon. When dough is firm enough to handle, knead gently. Form into 4 balls and refrigerate overnight.

To prepare the pomegranate sauce, boil the juice on medium heat until reduced in half with a consistency resembling maple syrup. Store in the refrigerator until ready to use.

Heat the oven to 325°F.

To fill samosas, pinch the dough into balls that fit into the palm of your hand. Roll these out on a surface that has been powdered with arrowroot powder.

Place a few teaspoons of the filling into the center of each dough circle, then pull up the corners of the dough, forming a cone-like triangular shape. Seal the edges of the dough and brush with heating oil.

Place samosas on a baking sheet lined with baking paper, and place into the hot oven.

Bake for 45 minutes, checking often to brush on extra oil if the samosas are looking dry.

Serve the samosas with the pomegranate dipping sauce and nori dressing.

Marinated Baby Beans and Lentil Salad

Baby beans are a real treat in the summer months when hot days are followed by cool evenings. Baby beans cook much more quickly than mature beans, and are easy to cool and use the next day. A large bowl of cool baby bean and lentil salad with sea palm and kale brings nourishment to us even when it is too hot to stand near the stove to cook.

beans
> 1 pound dried mixed heirloom baby beans (look for lima, navy, white soldier, cranberry, black)
>
> 1 stick kombu
>
> 1 stick wakame

lentils
> 2 cups dried black, brown, or green lentils
>
> 2 cups light broth or water
>
> 1 bay leaf
>
> ¼ cup sage, chopped

salad
> ¼ cup onion, minced (optional)
>
> 1½ cups Sea Palm Salad Dressing (see page 25)
>
> 1 cup baby kale, chopped
>
> lots of fresh lemon thyme, stems removed
>
> ¼ cup parsley, chopped
>
> 3 tablespoons olive oil
>
> 1 teaspoon coarse salt

Soak the baby beans 12 hours, drain, rinse, and continue to soak an additional 12 hours.

Bring a large pot of water to boil with kombu and wakame. Add beans and boil for about half an hour, or until tender. Drain. Reserve wakame and set aside the kombu for another use.

Boil lentils with light broth, bay leaf, and sage for 5 minutes, lower heat, cover, and simmer on low heat for 20 minutes.

Combine beans, lentils, onion, Sea Palm Dressing, and kale. Remove and discard center rib from wakame, mince wakame, and add to the salad. Let marinate, refrigerated, for a minimum of 1 hour and up to 24 hours. Drain any extra liquid, then add thyme and parsley. Drizzle with olive oil, sprinkle with salt, and serve.

The Vegan Caesar

The original version of the Caesar salad is a classic example of "slow food" using artisanal ingredients. This recipe, in addition to using the best ingredients, is a celebration of differences, offering yet another way to truly share a meal.

dressing
   1 cup tahini
   2 cups lemon juice
   3 tablespoons umeboshi plum paste
   1 cup olive oil
   2 teaspoons garlic juice *or* 5 cloves garlic, pressed
salad
   2 heads romaine lettuce
   2 large handfuls dried dulse
croutons
   6 slices rice bread, toasted
   2 teaspoons olive oil
   1 teaspoon garlic juice *or* 4 cloves garlic, pressed
   1 teaspoon fine salt
   1 teaspoon black pepper, crushed

Combine tahini, lemon juice, plum paste, olive oil, and garlic. Whisk well, adding water if the mixture is too thick (it should pour freely).

To make the croutons, cut toast into $\frac{1}{2}$-inch squares. Combine olive oil, garlic, salt, and pepper, and toss or spray onto the toast cubes. Set aside or hold in a warm oven.

Wash the romaine leaves and drain. Cut into small pieces. Toss with the dressing.

Soak dulse briefly and remove from water when it is soft and pliable. Make sure it is free of sand or stones. Slice into thin strips.

Just before serving, toss the dulse and dressing with the romaine, and scatter with croutons.

Seawhip and Lotus Root Salad with Maple Sesame Dressing

The first time I had seawhip was in New Zealand. An Israeli friend brought me several strands of dried seawhip as a housewarming present. When he tried to describe the texture and flavor to me, I was completely intrigued and had to taste it. I'm still not sure how to describe the texture—it is somewhat meaty as far as sea vegetables go, and not very fishy-tasting. As soon as I tried the sea vegetable once, I knew that it would be complemented by my favorite condiments, sesame oil and maple syrup! If you live where seawhip grows, look for fresh seawhip (also known as bullwhip kelp). I urge you to collect even just one tender tube of it. Take it home, cut it into 1-inch lengths, string it up, and dry it before cooking.

> 2 cups dried seawhip, 1-inch lengths
> 4 inches lotus root, fresh, sliced thinly
> 2 tablespoons ginger juice
> 2 tablespoons maple syrup
> 2 tablespoons sesame oil
> 1 tablespoon wheat-free tamari
> ½ tablespoon rice vinegar

In a large pot of boiling water, simmer the seawhip for about an hour, or until it is tender and easily cut with a knife. Drain and let cool completely.

Combine all of the ingredients and serve.

The Vegan "Tuna" Salad

There are many versions of this vegan favorite. Kelp is a natural seasoning agent here, working well to bring flavors of the sea to a vegan menu.

> 1 12-ounce package tempeh with sea vegetables
> 1 carrot, steamed and chopped
> 1 cup celery, steamed and chopped
> ¼ cup onion, chopped (optional)

½ cup aioli (you choose the flavor—see pages 25–26)
1 teaspoon lemon juice
2 tablespoons kelp granules
black pepper

Fill a saucepan with water, and bring to a simmer over medium-high heat. Immerse the tempeh in the water, and simmer for 5 minutes. Remove from pan and let cool completely.

Combine the carrot, celery, onion, aioli, and lemon juice. Crumble tempeh with your hands and add to the celery and carrot mixture. Add kelp and black pepper, and stir until just combined. Serve with rice crackers and bullwhip pickles.

four

Soups

Chilled Heirloom Pea Soup with Seasoned Mochi Coins

This soup is a joyous celebration of early summer. Sweet, fresh peas are easy to grow and are abundant throughout the growing season. There are many different varieties of peas. Any combination will work in this recipe. Enjoy a casual outdoor meal with a friend starting with this refreshing and nurturing chilled soup.

> 6 quarts light broth (see pages 125–126)
> 8 cups shelled peas
> $\frac{1}{2}$ cup virgin olive oil
> freshly ground pepper
> *mochi coins*
> 1 package seeded mochi
> $\frac{1}{2}$ cup arame, soaked and drained
> 2 tablespoons prepared black sesame seeds
> 1 tablespoon Zesty Peck (optional—see page 20)
> 2 cloves garlic, pressed or grated
> $\frac{1}{4}$ cup heating oil
> Hawaiian black lava salt

Bring broth to a boil and add shelled peas. Return to a boil then lower heat and cook until peas are tender, approximately 15 minutes. Drain peas, saving broth. Run peas under cold water to preserve color. Set aside $\frac{1}{2}$ cup of peas. Blend remaining peas, olive oil, pepper, and broth with an immersion blender, or in a blender. Line a colander with a clean, thin, cotton tea towel, or several layers of cheesecloth, and strain the puréed mixture. Refrigerate immediately, until cool. Before serving, make the mochi coins.

Heat oven to 450°F.

With the grater attachment of a food processor, or with a box grater, grate mochi. Combine grated mochi, arame, sesame seeds, Zesty Peck, and garlic. Oil the wells of two muffin pans, and distribute mochi to a $\frac{1}{4}$-inch thickness.

Cook mochi until puffed and beginning to brown. Brush heating oil on top of the coins, sprinkle on salt, and return to oven until brown. (This total process should take less than 15 minutes.)

To serve, ladle the soup into bowls, distribute the whole cooked peas amongst the bowls, and drizzle on additional olive oil. Serve on a plate with mochi coins on the side.

Cool Asparagus Chowder with Black Sesame Sticks

This creamy, delicate soup is really more like a bright creamy broth than a chowder, but it has a fullness that creamy chowder boasts.

As a child, I was fortunate to know asparagus well. It grew in the grasses surrounding our vegetable garden, so we ate it regularly through the spring and early summer. Asparagus is easy to grow and is a perennial requiring little more than compost and patience (it takes two years until stable enough to harvest). It is worth the wait though, as every summer you will benefit from the freshest, most succulent, tender asparagus.

4 cups light broth (see pages 125–126)
4 cups chopped asparagus
$\frac{1}{4}$ cup chopped zucchini
$\frac{1}{4}$ cup chopped celery
$\frac{1}{4}$ cup chopped onion
$\frac{1}{4}$ cup chopped cucumber
2 cloves garlic, smashed
2 sprigs of thyme, stems removed
$\frac{1}{4}$ cup chopped flat parsley
$\frac{1}{2}$ cup organic virgin olive oil
2 tablespoons lemon juice
3 tablespoons wheat-free tamari or Bragg Liquid Aminos
garnish
$\frac{1}{4}$ cup fresh tarragon
1 tablespoon Meyer lemon oil or 1 tablespoon olive oil combined
with 1 teaspoon fresh lemon juice
$\frac{1}{2}$ teaspoon fleur de sal

black sesame sticks
   1 package seeded mochi
   ½ cup Nori Nettle Gomasio (see page 19)
   3 tablespoons Hawaiian black lava salt
   1 teaspoon finely grated lemon zest
   3 tablespoons heating oil

To make the chowder:

Bring the first nine ingredients to a boil, lower heat, cover, and simmer gently for 5–10 minutes until vegetables are tender. With a spoon, remove any foam that rises. Remove from heat. Add olive oil, lemon juice, and tamari or Braggs to vegetables and blend with an immersion blender or food processor until vegetables are blended thoroughly. Let mixture cool slightly. Line a colander with clean muslin or cheesecloth, and strain soup into another container. Discard any remaining solid bits. Season the soup with salt and fresh pepper to taste, and refrigerate until cool.

To make the garnish:

Macerate tarragon in a mortar or small spice processor. Add salt and oil until well combined. Refrigerate until ready to serve.

To make the black sesame sticks:

Heat oven to 450°F. Brush a cookie sheet with some heating oil. Mix gomasio, salt, and lemon zest. Spread evenly on a flat plate and set aside. Slice the mochi into ½-inch rods and place on the cookie sheet. Cook the mochi until just beginning to puff and bubble. Remove mochi from the oven, and brush with remaining heating oil. Carefully roll each stick in gomasio mixture, return to pan, and place back in oven. Continue cooking until the mochi is fully puffed, browned, and crispy (but not hard), about 2–5 minutes.

To serve the soup, first whisk or blend (with an immersion blender or hand mixer) to ensure the creamiest texture. Ladle soup into bowls, garnishing each with speckles of freshly ground pepper and the tarragon paste. Place black sesame sticks on top of bowl and serve.

Asian Meatballs in a Gingered Broth

In the coolness of autumn, this soup shines: silky meatballs in a nourishing broth that is simple yet well defined by the spiciness of ginger.

meatballs

1 pound local ground meat (white or red)

3 tablespoons arrowroot powder or white rice flour

2 tablespoons wheat-free tamari or Bragg Liquid Aminos

1 tablespoon ginger juice

½ cup minced coriander

1 onion, minced

3 cloves garlic, minced

1 tablespoon chopped wakame or alaria, central rib removed

½ cup rice flour

1 cup heating oil

⅛ cup additional wheat-free tamari or Bragg Liquid Aminos

⅛ cup mirin

1 lime

1 cup light broth (see pages 125–126)

3 sheets dried nori paper

broth

6 cups light broth

6 dried shiitake mushrooms

2 thumb-sized pieces of ginger, cut into slices

3 tablespoons miso (optional)

2 cups cooked rice pasta elbows (optional)

3 large shiso leaves *or* 1 bunch scallions to garnish

To make the meatballs, preheat oven to 350°F.

Combine meat, arrowroot, tamari, ginger juice, coriander, onion, garlic, and wakame. Mix well and roll into small walnut-sized balls. Dip or roll these balls in the rice flour. Heat the oil in a heavy skillet until it shimmers, or when a small portion of the meat will sizzle when dropped in. Fry the balls in the hot oil until brown on all sides and place in a baking dish.

Combine additional tamari and mirin and drizzle over meatballs. Squeeze in juice of lime and put lime rind in the pan as well. Roll nori paper into a tube shape and, with a pair of kitchen scissors, cut nori into thin strands and place on top of meatballs. Add 1 cup of light broth, cover and cook for 1 hour, or refrigerate until ready to cook.

Before serving, prepare broth with ginger and dried shiitake mushrooms. At this point heat either using a quick boiling method (boil for 10 minutes then reduce heat and simmer for 10) or a slow method (bring to a boil then reduce heat and cover, for ½ hour to 3 hours depending on your style). Reserve shiitake for another use, and discard ginger.

To serve, combine miso (if using) with broth. Ladle broth into bowls, place three or four meatballs in each bowl, a serving of pasta (optional), and garnish with thin slivers of shiso or scallions.

Basic Miso with Lotus, Ginger, and Burdock Roots

Consider this recipe when nothing else is appetizing, or when other foods are too difficult to digest. The roots in this recipe each offer different qualities. The lotus gives us purity in its whiteness and beauty in its form. The ginger offers spice, digestive stimulation, and flavor. The burdock is toning and purifying for the blood stream.

Miso is an ancient food excellent for times of healing as well as in times of transition. There are many different varieties based on a range of ingredients. Dark miso is best for the darker, colder months, while the lighter varieties are ideal in the longer light of warmer months.

2 tablespoons heating oil
6–10 inches of fresh burdock root, cut into matchsticks
1 thumb-sized piece of ginger, cut into rounds

4–6 inches of whole fresh lotus root, sliced into rounds

2 sticks kombu

6 cups water

⅛ cup miso (see side note)

wheat-free tamari or Bragg Liquid Aminos

sesame oil

cayenne (optional)

rice pasta elbows (optional)

Heat the oil in a heavy skillet and sauté the burdock until browned.

In a saucepan, boil the burdock, ginger, lotus root, and kombu. Reduce heat and simmer for about 15 minutes. Discard ginger and remove kombu. Ladle broth into a bowl and mix with miso until dissolved. Distribute miso broth amongst four bowls. Ladle remaining broth and roots into the bowls. Add tamari to taste, drizzle with sesame oil, and sprinkle on a wee bit of cayenne (optional). Add pasta elbows if using, and serve.

Shrimp Dumpling Drop Soup

Dumplings are always a treat! The extra bit of time it takes to prepare them is worth it, as guests (adults and children alike) are always impressed. This broth is simple yet supportive of the luxurious texture and flavor of the shrimp dumplings.

dumplings

1 pound fresh wild shrimp, shelled and cleaned

1 egg, or replacement

2 tablespoons tamari or Bragg Liquid Aminos

1 teaspoon fresh ginger juice

2 scallions, chopped

2 teaspoons sesame oil

2 teaspoons arrowroot powder

¼ teaspoon freshly ground black pepper

broth

6 cups fish broth

½ lemon

3 garlic cloves, bruised or smashed

1 thumb-sized piece of ginger, cut into rounds

1 cup arame, soaked

garnish

2 leaves minced shiso *or* several leaves of coriander

3 scallions, sliced

fresh horseradish (optional)

To make dumpling dough, first set aside one handful of shrimp. In a food processor, combine the next seven ingredients until you have a smooth paste. Add shrimp (minus the handful reserved) and process until smooth. Add remaining shrimp and pulse to mince but do not purée. Cover and refrigerate until just before serving the soup.

To make the broth:

In a saucepan, combine broth, lemon, garlic, and ginger. Simmer on medium, covered, for at least half an hour. Remove lemon, ginger, and garlic. Add arame and return to a simmer. Drop tablespoons of dumpling dough into the simmering broth, cover, and cook for about 3 minutes. Remove from heat and ladle into bowls, garnishing with additional tamari, shiso or coriander, scallions, and a generous grating of fresh horseradish (if using).

Wilted Amaranth in Garlic-Spiked Dashi

Amaranth is a native plant in the Americas. It has edible leaves, and its seeds are used as a grain and a flour. The tender young leaves of amaranth are red, bringing conversation and uniqueness to the table while quietly joining your menu with a subtle flavor much like spinach. If you are unable to find amaranth, first try asking a local farmer (it often grows as a weed), or look for the equally delectable native green lambsquarter. If you are still having a hard time, spinach works just fine.

¼ cup heating oil

10 cloves garlic

6 cups basic dashi (see page 125)

5 cups amaranth leaves, washed, stemmed, and barely chopped
salt
tamari or Bragg Liquid Aminos
freshly ground black pepper
3 tablespoons bonito flakes (optional)

In a heavy-bottomed saucepan, heat oil to almost smoking, toss in garlic, and fry until just beginning to brown. Remove from heat and drain the oil, reserving for later use. Add the dashi to the pot of cooked garlic, cover, and simmer on medium heat for at least half an hour. Remove garlic and crush with a spoon to achieve a smooth paste.

Just before serving, re-heat the oil in a skillet and when shimmering, toss in amaranth with salt and garlic paste. Cook the greens until just wilted, and remove from heat.

To serve, mound the greens in four serving bowls. Add a dash of tamari and ladle broth around each mound. Top with fresh black pepper and bonito flakes (if using).

Chrysanthemum Blossom Soup

Like lavender and chamomile, chrysanthemums offer subtle healing properties in the form of fragrant flowers. The petals of the chrysanthemum are cooling and toning, and are used by many to treat a variety of infections. These nurturing and cheering flowers are perfect for sharing in this spring or summer soup.

¼ cup dried chrysanthemum flowers soaked in 1 cup water
4 cups basic dashi (see page 125)
2 tablespoons mirin
3 tablespoons tamari or Bragg Liquid Aminos
1 cup thinly sliced baby bok choy or other baby Asian greens
½ cup fresh baby peas (removed from pod)

Soak flowers for 15 minutes then pull petals from center part and stem; reserve petals and soaking liquid.

In a saucepan or small pot, heat dashi, mirin, tamari, petals, and the soaking liquid. Bring to a simmer and reduce heat. Add bok choy and peas, cover, and continue to heat on low until peas and greens are tender (about 5 minutes). Ladle into bowls and enjoy!

Oaxaca Beans with Flatbread

There are so many different kinds of beans, and every year it seems that new heirloom varieties make it to the market. Kombu helps beans to become more easily digestible and adds flavor to basic bean recipes. Experiment with different types of beans, but always be sure to allow enough time for proper soaking and cooking.

> 2 cups dried beans
> 5 pieces kombu
> ½ pound local organic ground or stew meat (optional)
> 1 onion
> 2 cloves garlic, sliced
> 3 tablespoons paprika (optional)
> 2 tablespoons cumin
> 1 teaspoon black pepper
> 1 bunch scallions
> 1 bunch coriander, washed
> salt to taste
> 1 lime
>
> *flatbread*
> 1 package garlic mochi, sliced in thin strips
> 3 tablespoons heating oil
> ⅛ cup Pumpkin Seed Crust mixture (see page 23)
> 2 cloves garlic
> solar-dried sea salt
>
> *garnish*
> Lime Cumin Aioli (see page 26)
> 1–2 avocados

Soak the beans 12 hours, drain, rinse, and continue to soak an additional 12 hours.

To cook the beans you can either:

1) Use a slow cooker:
Cover beans with water. Add the next seven ingredients and cook on medium for up to 10 hours. Add scallions and coriander in the last half hour of cooking.

or

2) In a tall pot on the stove:
Boil beans and the following seven ingredients in lots of water (enough to cover and then three inches) for about 2 hours. Turn off heat and add coriander and scallions. Let rest for half an hour before serving. Remove kombu, salt to taste.

To make flatbread:

Heat oven to 450°F.

Lightly brush some heating oil on a baking sheet. In a small bowl, combine Pumpkin Seed Crust mixture and remaining heating oil. Press garlic through a garlic press into this mixture. Set aside.

Just before serving beans, place mochi slices flat on the baking sheet in groups of six to eight, leaving spaces between groups. When mochi is heated it will melt, forming hand-sized flatbreads. Place in the oven and cook until mochi has begun to puff up, then gently brush or sprinkle on pumpkin seed and garlic mixture and return to oven until mochi is brown and bubbly. (Total cooking time should be under 10 minutes.) Flatbreads should be eaten immediately.

Ladle beans and broth into bowls. Garnish with diced avocado, lime juice, and a spoonful of aioli. Serve with flatbreads.

Roasted Salmon Dumplings in Miso with Sizzling Rice

This recipe yields beautiful golden packages full of bright pink salmon and sexy black sea vegetables. The bowls seem to sparkle with the sizzled rice, which is immersed in a simple broth accented by the health-promising characteristics of miso and ginger. This recipe is perfect for advance preparation. Bake the salmon and cook the rice ahead of time, saving the final steps for just prior to serving.

    1 cup cooked brown rice
    1 pound wild salmon

    juice of 1 lemon
    1 tablespoon maple syrup *or* brown rice syrup
    $\frac{1}{2}$ teaspoon ground red pepper *or* a pinch of
        cayenne
    salt
    10 cloves garlic (optional), peeled
    1 cup sea palm, soaked
    $\frac{1}{2}$ cup water

    large Thai rice paper wrappers
    4 cups basic dashi (see page 125)
    1 tablespoon ginger juice
    heating oil
    miso
garnish
    sesame oil
    wheat-free tamari or Bragg Liquid Aminos to taste
    4–6 scallions

To cook the salmon:

Heat oven to 250°F.

Place the salmon in a baking dish. Combine lemon juice, syrup, cayenne, and salt. Pour mixture on top of fish. Place garlic cloves, sea palm, and water in the pan. Bake for 1$\frac{1}{2}$ hours or until salmon is cooked all the way through. Remove from heat. Cool slightly. Remove and discard bones. Remove garlic and sea palm and process or blend until you have a smooth paste. Spread this paste on the salmon and return to the oven, this time placed under the broiler. Broil until the top is beginning to look crispy and is bubbling. Remove from the oven and cool completely.

To make the dumplings:

Prepare a wrapper by placing in cool water until soft and pliable (about 2 minutes). Remove from the water, drying extra moisture on a tea towel. Place a spoonful of salmon on the edge of the wrapper and fold the paper. First fold in the edges, then roll until you have a square-shaped bundle. Repeat. In a heavy skillet, heat oil until shimmering, and fry the dumplings a few at a time. When one side is brown, add ¼ cup of cooked brown rice, scattering it throughout the pan. Add a few drops of tamari. The rice should stick to the dumplings. Continue to fry until evenly brown.

To make the soup:

Heat dashi and ginger juice on medium. Remove from heat just before serving, and add miso. Place two dumplings in each bowl. Ladle broth around dumplings. Garnish with sesame oil and tamari to taste. Scatter sliced scallions on top.

Coconut Fish Curry with Pumpkin and Plum Sauce

The Asian flavors here have all of the keynotes: hot, sour, salty, and sweet. In the summer add additional lemon or lime juice, and in the winter add a cinnamon stick for warmth and depth.

soup
   3 cups light broth (see pages 125–126)
   1 lemongrass stalk, split and bruised, *or* 1 lemon, seeds removed
   1 teaspoon ground red peppercorns or Szechuan peppercorns
   2 thumb-sized pieces of ginger, sliced
   ½ red kuri pumpkin (alternatively use: kobucha, blue hubbard,
      acorn, or butternut squash), skin and seeds removed,
      sliced into long thin strips
   1 tablespoon ginger juice
   1 tablespoon fish sauce *or* 1 tablespoon anchovy paste mixed
      with ½ tablespoon water (optional)
   juice of 1 lemon or lime
   2 teaspoons maple syrup

tamari or Bragg Liquid Aminos to taste

1½ cups coconut milk

6 shiitake mushrooms, thinly sliced

1 pound bok choy, chopped into small slices

1 tablespoon heating oil

tempura

1 pound wild, white, firm fish (snapper, cod, etc.), bones removed, and broken into large pieces.

1 cup rice milk

1 cup heating oil

1 cup white rice flour

1 teaspoon fine salt

¼ cup arrowroot (optional)

1 cup soaked sea palm fronds

plum sauce

about 15 ripe juicy plums, pits removed

3 cloves garlic, bruised or smashed

2 tablespoons grated ginger

1 teaspoon Szechuan peppercorns, slightly crushed, *or* 1 tablespoon fresh ginger juice

1 cup honey

1 tablespoon lemon juice

½ teaspoon additional peppercorns

salt to taste

3 cups cooked jasmine rice (optional)

To make the plum sauce:

Gently boil plums, garlic, ginger, and peppercorns together in a covered pot for about 40 minutes. Remove from heat and cool. Strain in a mesh strainer, pressing the juices through. Incorporate honey, lemon juice, and ½ teaspoon additional peppercorns into strained mixture and blend with an immersion blender. Refrigerate until set.

To make the soup:

Bring broth, lemongrass, pepper, and ginger to a slow boil. Cover, and simmer for at least 20 minutes. Add the pumpkin and continue to simmer for 10 minutes. Mix the ginger juice, fish sauce, lemon juice, and maple syrup in a small bowl. Add tamari and taste. The mixture should be hot, sour, salty, and sweet. This is a condensed version of what the broth will be. Add this mixture to the broth. Lower heat to lowest setting. Remove lemongrass, pepper, and ginger from the pot. In a hot skillet, melt the heating oil and quickly fry mushrooms and bok choy. Pour into broth and cover. Remove from heat.

To make fish tempura:

Preheat oven to 300°F.

Soak the fish in rice milk. Combine rice flour, salt, and arrowroot. In a cast-iron skillet, heat oil on high until shimmering, then lower heat to medium, testing occasionally, to be sure oil is at frying temperature (a vegetable dropped in will sizzle and bubble at a moderate rate). Dip fish into rice flour mixture, coating evenly, then place in hot oil. Brown each side evenly. Repeat until each piece is fried. Place fried fish into a baking dish. Place sea palm in dish between fish pieces, and drizzle with plum sauce. Place in preheated oven and bake for 20 minutes.

To serve, pour coconut milk into the soup and heat gently until just steaming. Ladle soup into bowls, distributing pumpkin, mushrooms, and greens evenly. Spoon a mound of rice (if using) into the center of each bowl, place pieces of fish on rice, and top with several strands of sea vegetables. Drizzle plum sauce on the outer edges of the soup.

A Summer Chicken Soup with Sea Palm, Rosemary, and Lemon

This is a hot soup that is also light and tangy, with hints of something wild and complex.

> 2–3 pounds chicken legs and/or thighs
> 2 heads fresh summer garlic
> 3 stems fresh rosemary

small bunch of lemon or regular thyme
2 Meyer lemons (or 1 large lemon)
8 cups light broth (see pages 125–126)
1 cup sea palm fronds
2 small summer heirloom carrots, cut in thin rounds
1 cup cauliflower fronds
½ cup young rainbow chard, chopped
extra virgin olive oil
2 tablespoons fresh rosemary, stems removed, and minced
salt to taste
freshly ground black pepper

Preheat oven to 300°F.

In a braising pan or oven-proof dish with a tight-fitting lid, place chicken, garlic, herbs (minus minced rosemary at end of ingredient list), lemon, and 2 cups of broth. Put in oven and cook for 2 hours. Remove pan from oven and carefully remove lid. Remove chicken and garlic from the dish to a rack placed over a cookie sheet to halt cooking and encourage it to cool down. Discard the green herbs and lemon. Pour remaining liquid over sea palm in a separate bowl. When garlic is cool enough to handle, squeeze cloves into sea palm. Remove and discard chicken skin, and separate meat from bones. In a large pot, heat remaining broth combined with chicken meat, carrots, and cauliflower. Bring to a boil, lower heat, and simmer for 10 minutes. Add chard and sea palm. When chard is bright in color, remove soup pot from heat and serve in bowls, drizzled with olive oil and sprinkled with minced rosemary and freshly ground pepper.

Fresh Scallop Noodles in a Lemongrass Broth

In cities and villages throughout Asia, home cooks and professional noodle makers create fine pastas from a variety of local ingredients including non-glutinous pure buckwheat flour, as they have done for centuries. These scallop noodles are a reflection of this tradition, as well as the gifts of the sea. They are hearty and succulent, grain-free, and so easy to make.

noodles

> 1 pound fresh scallops, patted dry (or fresh shrimp, cleaned
> and dried) *or* 1 pound soft tofu mixed with 1 teaspoon agar
> powder and 1 teaspoon arrowroot
> 2 egg whites (*or* 2 tablespoons freshly ground flax seed
> mixed with 5 tablespoons water)
> ½ teaspoon agar powder
> 1 tablespoon mirin
> 2 teaspoons wheat-free tamari or Bragg Liquid Aminos

soup

> 6 cups light broth (see pages 125–126)
> 2 stalks lemongrass (*or* 2 lemons, seeds removed)
> ½ tablespoon pink peppercorns or mixed peppercorns
> 2 cups chopped tsatsoi or bok choy
> 2 tablespoons fish sauce
> 2 tablespoons ginger juice
> 1 teaspoon crushed red peppercorns *or* 1 teaspoon
> red chili paste (optional)
> 1 teaspoon tamari or Bragg Liquid Aminos to taste

garnish

> 3 sheets nori, cut into thin shreds
> 2 tablespoons mirin
> 1 tablespoon tamari or Bragg Liquid Aminos
> 2 tablespoons heating oil
> ½ cup chopped scallions
> sesame oil

To make the noodles:

Mince scallops (or shrimp, or tofu mixture) in a food processor. Add egg whites (or flax mixture), agar, mirin, and tamari, and process until it is a smooth paste. Transfer into a plastic bag and store in refrigerator for at least one hour.

To make the broth:

Heat broth, lemongrass (or lemons), and peppercorns together in a large pot. Bring to a slow boil, reduce heat, and gently simmer while covered. Meanwhile, on high heat, quickly stir-fry tsatsoi (or bok choy) until slices just begin to lose moisture. Pour greens, fish sauce, ginger juice, peppercorns, and tamari into the broth. Set heat to the lowest setting, and prepare the noodles.

To cook the noodles:

Bring a large pot of salted water to a boil. Snip the corner of the plastic bag to resemble a pastry bag (or use a pastry bag with a medium tip). Secure top of bag, and gently squeeze paste into boiling water and cook for 1 minute. Remove noodles with a large slotted spoon, drain, and continue with remaining paste.

For the garnish:

Just before serving, heat a frying pan on high. Melt the cooking oil and when shimmering, add nori strips, mirin, and tamari. Fry nori for 2–3 minutes, or until crisp; set aside.

To serve, place several noodles in each bowl. Ladle the broth over the noodles, distributing the tsatsoi evenly. Top each bowl with a sprinkling of scallions, a drizzle of sesame oil, and a tangle of fried nori.

five

Mains

Chicken and Arame with Deep Chocolate Hazelnut Picada

Anything with chocolate has to be good! When chocolate is treated as a special food, like saffron or wild mushrooms, we give ourselves an opportunity to truly taste and experience its flavors. Bring something dark and mysterious to the table! Serve with dark black beluga lentils (use French indigo lentils if you can't find the black) and dark greens.

Side note: There are two ways you can prepare this dish, I prefer this slower version, but you can definitely speed it up a little if you need to by omitting the braising technicality and simply simmering the chicken before adding the picada.

chicken
  2 pounds raw chicken pieces, bones and skin removed
  1 tablespoon olive oil
  1 tablespoon heating oil
  1 onion, chopped
  3 cloves garlic, pressed
  ½ cup tomatillos, chopped
  4 cups light broth (see pages 125–126)
  ½ cup dried arame
  ¼ cup dried hijiki
  ¼ cup lemon juice
  1 teaspoon sal gris

picada
  1 cup prepared hazelnuts, skin removed
  3 tablespoons very dark chocolate, chopped or grated,
     at room temperature
  3 cloves garlic
  ½ cup flat parsley, washed
  ¼ cup fresh cilantro, washed

    1 teaspoon grated orange zest
    ¼ teaspoon nutmeg

Heat oven to 300°F.

To cook the chicken:

In a large braising pan or a skillet, melt oil and cook onion until transparent. Brown chicken at high heat until evenly brown. Add garlic, tomatillos, and broth. Bring to a simmer. Add arame, hijiki, lemon juice, and sal gris. Remove from heat. Cover, or place in a baking dish that can be covered tightly, and cook for 2½ hours. (Alternatively, at this point you can simmer, uncovered, for half an hour or until the chicken is done and the liquid is reduced.)

To make the picada:

Process the hazelnuts in a food processor until smooth. Add remaining ingredients and process until smooth. Transfer to a bowl and set aside.

Before serving, remove chicken from the oven. Remove lid and place pan on a low burner. In small batches, stir picada into chicken and sea vegetables until all of the picada is incorporated. Serve with dark lentils and steamed greens.

Venison Medallions with Elderberry Hijiki Crust

An invitation into the wilderness, this dish is really about honoring the richness of the wild. The colors are royal with reds, purples, and black, like the forests in the end of autumn. There are few ingredients, but each brings a wealth of flavor. Venison, elderberries, hijiki, shallots, and sal gris are equally wild and mysterious and complement each other well. Serve this dish with wilted braising greens and prepared pecans, or steamed baby kale and mashed or roasted cauliflower with truffle oil, for the perfect autumn feast.

    2 pounds venison loin
    3 cups elderberries (or blueberries or huckleberries)
    3 tablespoons heating oil
    sal gris, or Celtic gray salt
    freshly ground pepper

6 shallots, sliced

1 cup hijiki, ground

1 cup hijiki, soaked (measure first)

Marinate venison and elderberries overnight, if time allows.

Heat oven to 400°F.

Melt oil in a skillet on high heat. Fry shallots until beginning to turn translucent; remove from pan and set aside. Remove venison from marinade (reserve berries) and sear until brown on all sides. Remove from heat, and cover with salt and pepper. Blend shallots with berries and whole and ground hijiki. Cover venison with mixture and place in oven. Cook for about 20 minutes. Remove from oven. Rest meat for about 10 minutes. With a very sharp knife, slice into medallions and serve.

Succulent Tofu with Seven Spices and Seaweed

This is an easy vegan dish and is a traditional tofu recipe. For those avoiding soy, the tofu can be replaced by any meat or firm mushroom for a luscious spicy Szechuan treat. Serve with your favorite rice and sautéed Asian greens, mustard greens, or chard.

sauce

1½ tablespoons arrowroot mixed with ¾ cup water or broth and

⅛ cup tamari, Bragg Liquid Aminos, or additional broth

tofu

⅛ cup heating oil

2 pounds tofu, pressed and cubed

2 cloves garlic, smashed

1 tablespoon ginger juice

3 whole star anise

½ cup hijiki, soaked

⅛ cup Seven Spices blend (see page 19)

3 tablespoons shiso, minced (optional)

3 scallions, chopped

sesame oil

Preheat oven to 400°F.

Melt oil in an oven-proof skillet on high heat. When oil is shimmering and only just beginning to smoke, add tofu. Lower heat if tofu seems to brown too quickly. Add garlic, ginger, star anise, and hijiki. Continue to fry until tofu is evenly browned. Remove from heat and stir in sauce (arrowroot mixture). Place in the oven and bake for 20 minutes. Remove from the oven and toss Seven Spices blend with tofu, coating evenly. Return to the oven for an additional 10 minutes. Discard the star anise and transfer to a serving platter. Top with shiso and scallions, and season with sesame oil.

Pan-Seared Salmon with Sea Palm

This basic recipe is a standard on the Northern California coast, where sea palm and salmon both live wild in abundance. The colors are fantastic, and the flavors are wholesome, fresh, and unique. But best of all, this recipe can be made in a flash with minimal ingredients. Quick and simple!

  1 lemon, seeds removed
  2 tablespoons heating oil
  1 pound wild salmon fillet
  2 cloves garlic, minced
  1 shallot, sliced
  2 cups sea palm
  1 cup water

Slice the lemon in half lengthwise, reserving one half. Slice the other half into thin half-rounds. Heat a heavy skillet to medium-high heat with oil. When oil is hot, place salmon skin side down in pan and sear for about 8 minutes. Turn salmon; add lemon slices, garlic, and shallot to the pan; and cover for about 8 minutes. Turn salmon again and place sea palm in pan around salmon. Add water and simmer. The sea palm should absorb all of the moisture in the pan. With a fork, continually stir and flip sea palm and lemon slices. When water is absorbed and sea palm is tender, remove from heat. Squeeze remaining half lemon on salmon. Serve with quinoa or seared zucchini and fresh summer peas.

Chicken Cacciatore

For those who imagine Italian food with "traditional" tomato sauce, I encourage you to contemplate Italy before tomatoes were introduced from South America. Then, if you can, think of Italy before the influence of the Asian noodle! Cacciatore is a collaborative dish, one that combines essences of the forest, the garden, the field, and now (with sea vegetables) the ocean. You won't miss the tomato sauce here, as the lemon juice, chicken, and sea palm collectively inspire a complex taste similar to parmesan-laden tomato sauce.

2 pounds chicken breasts and/or thighs

1 tablespoon heating oil

2 cloves garlic

1 cup wild mushrooms, minced

2 cups light broth

2 cups sea palm

1 stem rosemary

½ cup flat-leaf parsley, chopped

2 leaves sage

2 tablespoons fresh lemon thyme, minced

1 teaspoon salt

1 teaspoon ground pepper

1 lemon, seeds removed

2 tablespoons olive oil

Preheat oven to 300°F.

In a heavy skillet, melt oil and sear chicken, browning on all sides. Add garlic, mushrooms, and broth to the pan and bring to a simmer. Remove from heat. Add sea palm, rosemary, parsley, sage, lemon thyme, salt, and pepper. Squeeze lemon juice into the pan, then place remaining lemon rind in the pan as well. Cover and place in oven. Cook for 1 hour, then remove from oven and uncover. Drizzle olive oil into the pan and let rest for 5 minutes. Serve with steamed kale and a side of well-cooked white beans.

Baked Chicken with Sea Palm and Truffled Cauliflower

Again, the ingredients here rely on each other to produce a complex finished flavor. This meal is simple and sturdy, it is reliable, and will bring nourishing comfort to anyone who shares your table.

¼ pound sea palm or soaked wakame, center rib removed
1 cup water
1 whole chicken (about 4 pounds)
2 oranges or 1 pound kumquats, thinly sliced and seeds removed
2 apples, one thinly sliced, seeds removed
½ cup fresh sage, stems removed, rolled and chopped
1 cinnamon stick
pink table salts
pink peppercorns, ground, or mixed peppercorns
black pepper, ground
1 head cauliflower, cut into large pieces
truffle oil

Heat oven to 350°F.

Cover the bottom of a baking dish with sea palm and water, making way in the center for the chicken to sit. Place chicken in the baking dish, breast on top. Carefully slide your fingers between the skin of the chicken and the breast meat, separating the skin in the center and creating a pocket that reaches to the drumstick, if possible. Carefully insert slices of apples and oranges into this pocket, along with some of the chopped sage. Fill the pocket as much as possible. Place the cinnamon stick in the cavity of the chicken, along with the whole apple and any remaining orange slices.

Season the outside of the chicken with the salt, pink and black pepper, and any remaining sage. Place the cauliflower around the chicken. Bake for about 2 hours, basting the cauliflower and the chicken every half hour or so.

To serve, remove chicken from oven and let rest for about 15 minutes. Place sea palm on plates and top with slices of chicken. Place cauliflower next to chicken and drizzle with truffle oil. Ladle a bit of juice from bottom of pan onto chicken and serve.

Roast Lamb with Mint, Arame, and Kumquat Jam

Just as slow-roasted, baked, and braised meats are ideal in the cold winter months, basic seared or steamed meats are ideal in the summer. As the seasons shift, it is important to adapt to the changes. The time and methods used to prepare foods during different seasons are just as important as the foods consumed during those months of the year. Fresh lamb becomes available in the early summer. Mint, sea vegetables, and kumquats are also abundant during this time.

lamb and marinade
 about 2½ pounds thick-cut lamb chops or
  small boneless leg of lamb
 ⅛ cup Spice of Amazigh (see page 21)
 2 Medjool dates, seeds removed
 2 cloves garlic
 ¼ cup arame
 ¼ cup mint leaves, shredded
jam
 2 cups kumquats, sliced, seeds removed
 1 cup apple cider or pear juice
 ½ teaspoon stevia
 ½ cup brown rice syrup (optional)
 pinch of fine salt

To prepare marinade, first blend Spice of Amazigh, dates, garlic, arame, and half of the mint leaves in a blender or food processor. Cover lamb with mixture, place in a covered container, and refrigerate for at least 4 hours (and up to 2 days). Allow lamb to rest at room temperature prior to cooking.

To make the kumquat jam:

Simmer kumquats with apple cider, stevia, salt, and brown rice syrup (if using) on medium heat until liquid is reduced to a thick syrup and kumquat rinds are soft. Blend slightly with an immersion blender or in a food processor. The texture should resemble orange marmalade. Store in the refrigerator until ready to use.

To cook the lamb:

Prepare the grill or fire, and have reserved mint handy. Wipe excess marinade off lamb, and season with salt. Grill on a medium to high fire for about 5–7 minutes on each side. Sprinkle with the reserved mint before serving. Serve with spicy summer greens such as arugula, mizuna, or brassica greens and a drizzling of kumquat jam.

Arame Almond-Crusted Quail with Apricot Sauce and Autumn Greens

Quail is dark and wild-tasting, with a personality suited to sweet and tart flavors like berries, citrus, and apricots. You can easily use the game birds such as pheasant, game hens, duck, or spring chickens in place of the quail. Also feel comfortable using either whole birds or boneless fillets, and adjust the cooking time accordingly.

sauce
- 3 cups fresh apricots, pits removed then diced, *or* 1½ cups dried apricots soaked in equal amount of water
- 1 cup light broth
- fine salt

quail
- 4 one-pound quail
- 2 apples, halved
- 1 apple thinly sliced
- 1 tablespoon lemon thyme, minced
- 1 teaspoon minced sage
- 1½ cups prepared almonds, ground
- 1 cup arame, ground
- 1 cup apple cider or water
- 8 carrots, washed and cut in half, then quartered

- 4 cups braising greens
- freshly ground black pepper

Preheat oven to 350°F.

To make the apricot sauce:

Simmer apricots (and soaking water, if using) with broth on medium-low heat for about 15 minutes, or until reduced. Purée with an immersion blender or food processor, and salt to taste. Set aside until ready to use.

To cook the quail:

If using whole quail, gently separate the skin from the breast, and fill this space with several slices of apple and minced lemon thyme and sage. Fill center cavity of the bird with halved apple pieces. In a large bowl, combine almonds, arame, and apple cider or water. Place a quail into bowl and cover with almond mixture. Place each bird into a baking pan, and nestle the carrots between. Bake for about 15–25 minutes. (If using smaller fillets, roast the carrots separately for about half an hour and cook the meat for only about 10–15 minutes.)

Just before serving, heat the apricot sauce. Add water if sauce has become too thick. Toss greens with a small bit of this hot sauce, allowing them to wilt gently.

Place a mound of greens on each plate, topped with the roasted carrots and quail. Drizzle quail with remaining apricot sauce and sprinkle with freshly ground pepper.

Jasmine-Cured Pork in a Blended Seaweed Crust

This recipe asks you to let the pork cure for two days in a brine, which is something few people do anymore since it is easy to find pork already cured. Curing the pork in jasmine water gives a unique flavor to a holiday favorite. Serve this colorful dish with baked sweet potatoes and Asian mustard greens.

Curing the pork:
    4 pounds of pork—boneless shoulder or butt
    2 quarts boiling water
    2 oranges, seeds removed
    2 cups dried jasmine flowers

> 1 cup coarse sea salt
> 1 cup rice vinegar
> 1 cup mirin

Pour boiling water over oranges, jasmine, salt, vinegar, and mirin. Let steep all day or overnight. Strain into a large bowl or pan. Reserve orange and return to liquid. Place the pork into this brine. Add enough cold water to cover the meat completely. Cover and refrigerate for two full days.

Cooking the pork:

Combine:

> 2 tablespoons lemon or orange zest
> 1 cup ground arame
> 1/4 cup ground sea palm
> 1/4 cup ground hijiki

Preheat oven to 300°F.

Remove pork from brine and place it in a baking pan. Score the top of the meat in a criss-cross pattern. Evenly distribute half of the ground sea vegetable mixture. Let rest for about an hour. Place into the oven. Cook for 2 hours, basting every 15 minutes or as necessary. During the last 15 minutes, sprinkle remaining sea vegetable powder onto pork. Remove from oven and let rest for about 10 minutes before serving.

Vegan To-Furkey with Brown Rice and Amaranth Stuffing and Miso Gravy

The To-Furkey continues to be a novelty amongst the health-conscious. Even if you think that it's a silly idea, I encourage you to try this at least once. It is a GREAT meal to have the kids help make, as there is no scare of cross-contamination, and kids always love to make anything that is stuffed. Go on—you'll love it! If you are avoiding soy, use any variety of winter squash or pumpkin instead of the tofu shell (renaming it Squ-Furkey or Pum-Furkey, accordingly!). This recipe serves 4–6.

stuffing

    1 stem celery, finely chopped

    1 small onion, finely chopped

    2 cloves garlic, minced

    ½ cup mushrooms, finely chopped (optional)

    1 tablespoon heating oil

    1½ cups cooked brown rice

    1 cup cooked amaranth

    1 tablespoon fine orange zest

    ½ cup soaked arame

    ½ cup water

    1 small apple, diced

    ½ cup parsley, finely chopped

    2 teaspoons lemon thyme, minced

    2 tablespoons wheat-free tamari or Bragg Liquid Aminos

tofu

    4 pounds fresh firm or extra firm tofu, pressed and drained

    1 teaspoon agar powder

    1 tablespoon fresh summer savory, or 1 teaspoon dried

    2 tablespoons Zesty Peck (see page 20)

    2 tablespoons arrowroot powder

    1–3 tablespoons water

    2 tablespoons wheat-free tamari or Bragg Liquid Aminos

    ½ cup dashi (see page 125)

    2 shallots, roasted

gravy

    3 tablespoons arrowroot powder

    3 cups dashi or vegetable broth

    wheat-free tamari or Bragg Liquid Aminos to taste

    1 cup mushrooms, diced (optional) *or* 1 tablespoon dried shiitake
       mushrooms ground into a powder (optional)

    ⅛ cup miso

    freshly ground pepper

    2 tablespoons sesame oil

To make the stuffing, sauté celery, onion, garlic, and mushrooms in heating oil on medium-high heat until the onions are translucent. Add rice, amaranth, orange zest, arame, and water. Cook until the liquid is absorbed. Remove from heat and add apple, parsley, thyme, and tamari. Set aside.

Preheat oven to 350°F and line a baking dish with baking paper.

To prepare the tofu base, use a food processor to crumble the tofu. Add the agar, savory, Zesty Peck, and arrowroot and blend well. With the processor running, slowly add enough water until the tofu mixture is smooth.

Line a small colander with cheesecloth or muslin. Pour two-thirds of the tofu mixture into the lined colander. Push tofu onto all sides as well as spread on the bottom to a thickness of $2/3$ of an inch and let rest for 15 minutes. Pour cooled stuffing into the tofu-lined colander and cover with remaining tofu mixture. Gently invert stuffed tofu into the baking dish and remove the cheesecloth. Pour tamari, dashi, and shallots into the pan as well, and place in oven. Bake for 1 hour, basting every 15 minutes with liquid from the bottom of the pan.

Before serving, make the gravy. Make a slurry with arrowroot, $1/2$ cup of the dashi, and tamari, and set aside.

Remove the shallots from baking pan and cook with mushrooms (if using) until mushrooms are cooked through. Add the rest of the dashi and mushroom powder (if using) and bring to a simmer on medium-high heat. When liquid has reached a simmer, lower heat and add arrowroot slurry, stirring constantly. The gravy will be cloudy at first, but as the arrowroot is heated it will thicken and turn clear again. Remove from heat. Add the miso and blend well, making sure that all of the miso is combined. Season with fresh pepper to taste.

Just before serving, drizzle To-Furkey with sesame oil.

Serve with baked sweet potatoes, roasted cauliflower, and steamed kale.

Dried alaria from Pacific Wildcraft, a family business.

My kids love sea vegetables, especially hijiki caviar.

Crystal Maderia

Dried jasmine flowers, for Jasmine-cured Pork (see page 81).

Crystal Maderia

Sea vegetable spices

Wild Atlantic kelp thrives in fast-flowing subtidal waters.

Edible seaweeds thrive on ledges that jut out above the water line
on the new- and full-moon tides.

Pacific Kelp is dried on lines before packaging.

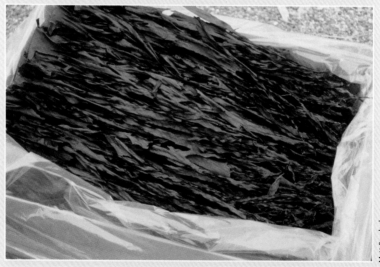

After complete drying, this kombu is ready to be
shipped in bulk to consumers.

Andrew and Tatiana of Pacific Wildcraft dry their sea vegetables inland where there is less fog and thus less moisture in the air. The sea vegetables dry quickly on screens in the shade.

Andrew of Pacific Wildcraft harvests sea palm.

Dried kombu strips and shiitake mushrooms

Sea Palm Straight Up

Edible flowers such as bachelor buttors (above) and calendula (below) add color, cheer, and light herbal flavors to spring and summer dishes.

Crystal Maderia

Crystal Maderia

Coriander flowers

Crystal Maderia

Johnny jump-ups

Crystal Maderia

Broiled White Fish Steaks with Seaweed and Anchovy Paste

Anchovy paste may sound unappetizing, but for centuries it has been relied on to bring depth and nutrition to the table. This sea vegetable paste is inspired by such efforts. You can cook the fish on a fire or a grill (my favorite) or under a broiler, or even in a cast-iron skillet on medium-high heat.

paste
   3 heads roasted garlic
   12 sheets Tangy Korean Nori, crumpled (see page 20)
   ¼ cup dry sea palm, ground into a powder (optional)
   2 teaspoons anchovy paste (optional)
   1 lemon, seeds removed

   4 servings wild-caught firm white fish such as sea bass or halibut

Squeeze the garlic into a bowl and discard the skin. Mix the Tangy Korean Nori, sea palm, and anchovy paste and stir until well combined.

Season the fish with lemon juice and sear one side of the fish for about 3 minutes. Gently turn, and while searing the other side spread the paste onto the top side of the fish. Cook for 3 minutes, covered. Remove from heat when the fish is flaky. Place the steaks under the broiler for an additional 2 minutes (optional).

Serve with lemon wedges and seared summer vegetables.

Fried Chicken in a Macadamia Crust with Honey-Lime Dipping Sauce

Occasionally fried food finds its way into our diet. This dish is inspired by the tropics, where fresh coconut oil, macadamia nuts, honey, and limes are all abundant. When summer temperatures soar, celebrate the heat, and share this dish for pleasure all around.

marinade
   ¼ cup fresh lemon juice
   ¼ cup mirin

   ½ teaspoon dried mustard powder

   ½ cup Dark Gingered Marinade (optional—see page 24)

   ½ teaspoon pink table salts

   3 pounds boneless chicken, cut into 1-inch-thick strips
      (and skewer-optional)

macadamia crust

   1 cup prepared macadamia nuts

   ¾ cup sea palm fronds

   2½ cups seasoned rice flour, *or* 1½ cups white rice flour mixed
      with 1 cup arrowroot and 1 teaspoon cayenne

   1 cup arrowroot powder

   4 eggs beaten, *or* 2 cups rice milk mixed with 3 tablespoons
      ground flax seeds

   2 cups coconut oil or heating oil

honey-lime dipping sauce

   ½ cup honey

   ½ cup lime juice

   2 tablespoons wheat-free tamari or Bragg Liquid Aminos

   2 tablespoons ginger juice

Combine the first five ingredients to marinate the chicken strips. Refrigerate at least 6 hours.

In a spice mill or food processor, process the macadamia nuts until they resemble a coarse flour. Add the sea palm, seasoned rice flour, and arrowroot powder. Pulse again a few times until well combined. Pour onto a plate or baking sheet.

To make the dipping sauce combine the honey, lime juice, tamari, and ginger juice and set aside until ready to serve.

Drain the chicken from the marinade, roll in the flour mixture, dip into the egg, then roll again in the flour mixture. Heat the coconut oil in a cast-iron skillet on medium heat. Test the oil by dropping a small piece of chicken into the oil, and if the chicken bubbles and begins to fry immediately, the oil is ready.

Fry the chicken in batches until golden and cooked through. Keep the cooked batches warm in a 200° oven until ready to serve.

For a party, serve with steamed sugar peas in the pod and slices of mango, grilled pineapple, or peaches.

Pumpkin Seed-Crusted Tofu with Steamed Garden Veggies and Plump Rice

This is a staple vegetarian dish. Simply change the veggies according to what is in season and use whatever rice you are inspired by at the moment. In the summer, use baby basmati rice or quinoa: they both cook quickly (thereby heating up the kitchen less in hot weather) and are good to have on hand when things get hectic. In the cooler months, use darker rice or risotto. Experiment and discover your own preferences.

tofu
   2 pounds firm fresh tofu, cubed
   2 tablespoons wheat-free tamari or Bragg Liquid Aminos
   2 teaspoons ginger juice
   1 cup Pumpkin Seed Crust (see page 23)
   2 tablespoons heating oil

lemon tahini sauce
   1 cup organic hulled tahini
   $\frac{1}{2}$ cup lemon juice
   $\frac{1}{8}$ cup wheat-free tamari or Bragg Liquid Aminos
   2 cloves garlic
   $\frac{1}{2}$ cup parsley, chopped
   1 cup water

veggies
   2 cups sliced red cabbage
   2 cups broccoli flowers
   2 large carrots, cut into matchsticks
   1 cup soaked arame or hijiki

2 cups cooked rice
flax seed oil (optional)
tamari to season

Marinate the tofu in ginger juice and tamari, and set aside.

To make the tahini sauce blend tahini, lemon juice, and Braggs in a blender. Add garlic and parsley and slowly drizzle in water while running the blender until sauce is thick, creamy, and speckled with green parsley. Set aside.

Steam cabbage, broccoli, carrots, and arame and set aside.

Drain the tofu and toss in the Pumpkin Seed Crust mixture until well coated. Melt heating oil in a cast-iron skillet on medium-high heat until shimmering. Pour the tofu into the pan and fry for 3 minutes. Turn and continue to fry until all sides are crispy and golden.

To serve, mound rice in the center of a bowl. Season with flax oil and/or tamari and top with the steamed veggies and tofu. Drizzle with the lemon tahini sauce.

Vegan Patty Party with Micro Greens, Tri-Colored Beets, and Aioli

Sunflower seeds, grains, and carrots are the main ingredients in this flexible and inexpensive recipe, perfect for feeding large groups of people or quick meals on the go. Make a large portion to have on hand, and freeze any extra patties for future use.

4 cups prepared sunflower seeds
3 cups cooked grains, any combination
2 cups grated carrots
¾ cup Kombu Shiitake Shake or Zesty Peck (see pages 24 and 20)
1 cup cooked beans or lentils (optional)
¼ cup flax seeds, ground
¼ cup wheat-free tamari or Bragg Liquid Aminos
red, gold, and spiraled beets, steamed, cooled, and sliced

>aioli of your choice (Vanilla Kombu, Lime Cumin, or Green
>   Peppercorn—see pages 25–26)
>baby salad greens or pea sprouts

In a food processor, finely grind the sunflower seeds in batches.

In a large bowl combine seeds, grains, carrots, and Kombu Shiitake Shake or Zesty Peck with lentils, flax, and tamari. In small batches, pulse this mixture in a food processor. When well combined, form into palm-sized patties.

To cook the patties, heat a cast-iron skillet and melt heating oil. Fry the patties on medium-low heat until each side is golden.

To serve, place several slices of steamed beets (all different colors) on each plate. Top the beets with some salad greens, then top with the patties and drizzle with aioli.

Store any leftover patty mix in the freezer. Reheat in a 300° oven for 15 minutes or until heated through.

six

Desserts

Whipped Cream

There are not many options for store-bought vegan whipped "cream," perhaps because it is difficult to create the same texture without the dairy fats, or the subtle sweetness without the natural sweetness of dairy. This recipe is a low-fat sugar-free variation that is great for dipping berries and serving with autumn pies.

>1 tablespoon agar flakes
>$\frac{1}{2}$ cup amazake
>1 cup silken soft tofu *or* $\frac{3}{4}$ cup vanilla amazake
>3 tablespoons brown rice syrup
>$\frac{1}{4}$ teaspoon stevia powder
>$\frac{1}{2}$ vanilla pod or 1 teaspoon extract

Soak agar in $\frac{1}{2}$ cup amazake for about 10 minutes, then bring to a boil, lower heat, and simmer on low for 15 minutes or until the agar dissolves. Blend tofu, brown rice syrup, and stevia until creamy, then add vanilla and agar-amazake mixture. Blend on low or with a whisk. Add salt to taste. Let cool in stages, whisking or gently blending occasionally to achieve a creamy consistency. Before serving, whisk or blend again.

Vegan Gluten-Free Cream Puffs with Berries

A favorite treat for children and adults alike, this simple dessert celebrates seasonal berries while providing comforting qualities of cream, crunch, and sweetness.

>whipped cream (see recipe above)
>2 cups berries (strawberries, blackberries, blueberries ...)
>
>1 cup egg replacer
>$\frac{3}{4}$ cup rice milk
>$\frac{3}{4}$ cup water
>$\frac{1}{4}$ teaspoon stevia powder

¼ cup sweet rice flour
¼ cup brown rice flour

Gently mash 1 cup of berries and set aside. Preheat oven to 450°F. Whip egg replacer, rice milk, water, and stevia until thick. Gently fold in the rice flours until combined. Scoop onto a cookie sheet with a teaspoon, and bake for about 10 minutes then lower oven to 350°F and bake an additional 15 to 20 minutes or until golden and cooked through (will sound hollow when tapped). Cool slightly, split open, fill with whipped cream, sprinkle with berries, and drizzle with remaining berry juice.

Vegan Marshmallows

Vegan marshmallows are available from an online distributor (see Sources), yet many people have asked how to make or where to buy them. This recipe is a treat for those who consider marshmallows a forbidden food.

3 tablespoons agar flakes
½ cup water
1 cup brown rice syrup
½ cup maple syrup
1 teaspoon stevia
¼ cup cold water
¼ teaspoon salt
seeds from one vanilla pod *or* 2 tablespoons extract

1 cup arrowroot powder mixed with 1 teaspoon stevia powder

Combine agar with ½ cup water and let soak for at least 1 hour. Separately combine the rest of the ingredients (excluding arrowroot) and bring to a boil (stay close to avoid boiling over). Boil for about 10 minutes, or until at a "firm ball" stage (meaning that the mixture turns into a firm ball when dropped into ice water). Remove from heat and pour slowly over the agar-water mixture and beat with an electric hand mixer for about 15 minutes or until the mixture shows thick globs.

Pour mixture into an 8x12 bread pan that has been dusted with arrowroot mixture. Dust the top with arrowroot mixture and set aside overnight (12 hours or so). Remove from the pan and cut the "marshmallows" into squares and dust each square with arrowroot mixture. At this point you can cut the squares again with a cookie cutter into alternative shapes (if desired), dust again, then store in an airtight container.

Butternut Cream

This "cream" is a healthful, not-too-sweet recipe that offers some variation in the fall, when pumpkin pie seems so prevalent. Use this recipe as a cake topping, pie filling, or serve frozen for ice cream.

> 4 cups baked butternut squash, skin removed
> 2 cups baked delicata, skin removed
> 1 cup apple juice
> 1½ tablespoons agar flakes
> 1 cinnamon stick
> ½ inch ginger, sliced
> 1 bruised vanilla pod
> ⅛ teaspoon fresh nutmeg shavings
> 1 cup amazake
> ¼ cup maple syrup
> 1 teaspoon stevia
> 1 tablespoon arrowroot
> ¼ teaspoon almond extract (optional)

Combine apple juice, agar, and spices in a large saucepan and bring to a boil, stirring constantly. Reduce heat and simmer gently for 20 minutes. Remove the cinnamon stick, ginger, and vanilla pod. Remove the seeds from the vanilla pod, and return seeds to the pot. Add the amazake, maple syrup, and stevia; return to a simmer.

Check that the agar is fully dissolved then add the squash and arrowroot. Using an electric mixer or immersion blender, blend the squash and liquid until continuously creamy. Bring again to a simmer and remove from heat. Add the almond extract now (optional). Pour the mixture into a bowl.

As the mixture cools, continue to blend, mix, or whisk, ensuring a smooth consistency. Blend or whisk again before using on a cake or pie. If you freeze the recipe, do so in a flat pan, freezing and whisking in stages, until thoroughly frozen, then mix again before serving.

Baked Figs with Honey Lemon Thyme Sorbet

Baked figs are a wondrous treasure—naturally sweet, soft, and luscious. Easily compared to a fine wine, the flavors in this dish are warm and spicy yet balanced with delightfully playful notes of herbs, honey, and fresh lemon.

> 1 Meyer lemon
> ½ vanilla pod
> 12 dried Mission figs
> ½ cup warm water
> ¼ teaspoon fleur de sal
> Honey Lemon Thyme Sorbet (see page 110)

Slice lemon in half, remove seeds, and squeeze juice into a bowl. Scrape vanilla seeds from pod and soak both with figs, lemon juice and peel, and ½ cup warm water. Soak overnight.

Preheat oven to 350°F. Bake the mixture, including the soaking liquid, uncovered for ½ hour, adding more liquid if figs seem dry. To make a syrup, more water is good, but too much will stew the figs. Remove from oven, cool slightly, sprinkle with fleur de sal, and serve warm with the sorbet.

Grilled Pineapple with Mint, Lime, and Coconut Ice Cream

Pineapples take a very long time to grow and are a very special treat for must of us. Celebrate the flavors of this miraculous fruit with equally magnificent flavors. Vanilla, mint, lime, and coconut unite to enhance the truly unique flavor of the grilled pineapple.

1 whole pineapple
1/2 vanilla pod
1/2 cup agave nectar
1/2 cup fresh mint
2 Key limes
Coconut Ice Cream (page 108)

Have ready a medium-hot grill. Hold the pineapple upright, and cut off the rind but not the top. Cut the pineapple in half and remove the central core. Set aside on a cookie sheet. Scrape the seeds of the vanilla pod into the agave nectar and simmer the pod with the nectar for 5 minutes on medium-low heat. Drizzle the nectar over the pineapple. Slice the vanilla pod in half down the center then into 8 lengths. Insert the vanilla into the pineapple by making slits in the pineapple at even intervals. Grill, rounded side down, for 15–30 minutes, depending on the intensity of the flame. Turn and sear the flat side for 5–10 minutes.

Meanwhile, crush the mint in a mortar until it resembles a paste but is not completely liquid. Remove the pineapple from the grill and allow to cool slightly. Cut one lime in half, and the other into 8 slivers; squeeze the halved lime over the pineapple. Cut the pineapple into equal portions, place on plates with ice cream, and serve with sprinkles of mint and a slice of lime.

Pecan Pie

This pie is a particularly nourishing treat in the autumn months. Delight in the extravagance!

1 pre-baked pie crust

1 tablespoon agar flakes
1/2 cup non-dairy milk
1/4 cup maple syrup
1/2 cup brown rice syrup
1/2 tablespoon fresh ginger juice or minced ginger
1 teaspoon cinnamon
1 1/2 cups coconut milk

    1 tablespoon arrowroot powder
    ¼ teaspoon stevia powder
    1 tablespoon vanilla extract
    2½ cups prepared pecans
    ¼ cup Medjool dates, pits removed, thinly sliced
    ¼ teaspoon salt
    1 stick soaked and minced kombu

Preheat oven to 350°F. Combine the agar flakes and non-dairy milk and bring to a simmer; stir and swirl the pan to keep the agar from sticking to the bottom. After 5 minutes add the maple and rice syrups, ginger, and cinnamon and bring to a simmer again, stirring constantly.

Mix a ½ cup of the coconut milk with the arrowroot and add to the pot. Stir and simmer on low for 2 minutes. Add the remaining coconut milk and continue to heat until nearly simmering. Add the stevia and remove from heat.

Add the vanilla and stir in the pecans, dates, salt, and kombu. Pour this mixture into the pie shell and bake for 20 minutes.

Lavender Lemon Pots of Cream

Cool, creamy, and sweet, this recipe has the qualities of a comfort food and is sensational. Look forward to making this dessert in the summer—it can be enjoyed cool or at room temperature. Either way, this dessert goes well with fresh-picked raspberries!

    1 vanilla pod, split lengthwise
    1½ cups amazake
    1½ cups rice milk (see page 124)
    2 teaspoons dried lavender flowers
    2 teaspoons agar
    ½ cup brown rice syrup
    ½ teaspoon stevia
    2 tablespoons arrowroot mixed with additional ¼ cup rice milk
topping
    ¼ cup brown rice syrup

¼ cup lemon juice

⅛ teaspoon stevia

Heat vanilla, amazake, rice milk, lavender, and agar in a saucepan until almost boiling. Reduce heat and simmer for 15 minutes on medium-low, stirring constantly. Add brown rice syrup and stevia, raise heat, and bring again to a near boil. Add the arrowroot mixture and stir constantly until it is dissolved completely. Cool 10 minutes in the pot at room temperature. Remove the vanilla, scraping any seeds that may remain in the pod back into the pot. Pour ½ cup into each individual serving container.

To make the topping:

Heat brown rice syrup until it begins to bubble in a heavy-bottom small cast-iron skillet. Add the lemon juice and stevia then simmer, while stirring, for 5 minutes. Drizzle topping over each serving, cover, and refrigerate.

Almond Nougat Panna

Almonds add a sturdy body to this creamy pudding, making it somewhat more filling than other custard recipes. This is a panna cotta for early fall, when the days are warm but the evenings are cool and wood smoke starts to fill the air.

½ cup brown rice syrup

2 cups almond amazake

1 cup almond milk (see page 123)

1 tablespoon agar

1 tablespoon arrowroot mixed with 3 tablespoons rice or almond milk

nougat

½ cup brown rice syrup

2 tablespoons ground almond paste (see page 123)

½ tablespoon arrowroot mixed with ⅛ cup almond milk

1 teaspoon vanilla extract

½ teaspoon almond extract

2 tablespoons chopped prepared almonds

Heat the first four ingredients until nearly boiling, reduce heat, and simmer, stirring for about 15 minutes. Raise the heat and when nearly boiling again, add the arrowroot mixture and stir about 2–4 minutes. Remove from heat; cool about 15 minutes.

To make the nougat, begin by bringing the brown rice syrup to a boil. Add the almond paste then the arrowroot mixture, whisking well to combine. Continue to simmer for 3–4 minutes then remove from heat. Add the extracts, whisk. Add chopped almonds and either pour over the top of individual servings of the panna cotta, or into the bottom of each serving container, then top with the cream. Cover and refrigerate.

Toffee Brittle

This not-too-sweet toffee is a fun conversation piece, and a treat celebrated by all. Use to decorate holiday plates, to accompany The Cake (page 104), sorbet, or ice cream, or to serve alongside a cup of tea. Vary the seeds or nuts depending on what you have on hand.

> 1½ cups brown rice syrup
> ½ cup toasted sea palm or toasted crushed nori
> ⅛–¼ cup prepared crushed pecans, almonds, pumpkin, sunflower, cumin, or sesame seeds (optional)

In a cast-iron skillet, bring brown rice syrup to a boil, stirring constantly. Reduce heat to medium and continue to simmer about 15 minutes. Add the sea vegetables and seeds (if using) and remove from heat. Immediately pour onto parchment paper. If the mixture is too thick or has cooled down too quickly to pour, heat it up again. You may need to add another teaspoon of brown rice syrup and bring to a boil again, then pour or drizzle immediately. Store in an airtight container.

Cheese and Figs

There are many recipes for vegan cheese. This particular variation is a sweet ricotta-like soy-free version perfect alongside fresh figs.

2 cups amazake

1 tablespoon roasted sesame tahini

2 tablespoons agar flakes

2 tablespoons arrowroot mixed with ½ cup rice milk and
    3 tablespoons lemon juice

½ teaspoon salt

date honey

4 Medjool dates

3 tablespoons dark honey

2 tablespoons warm water

12 fresh figs (strawberry or black Mission)

To make the cheese, combine amazake, tahini, and agar in a saucepan. Whisk until the tahini is well combined and bring to boil on medium-high heat, stirring continuously. Gently boil while stirring for about 10 minutes, until the agar is dissolved. Add the arrowroot mixture to the amazake mixture, stirring continuously until bubbles begin again. Remove from the heat, add the salt, and cool on the counter for about an hour.

Prepare the cheesecloth by draping it over a large-mouth jar or pitcher, or line a colander with it and place the colander over a larger bowl. When the amazake mixture is cool, whisk for about 3 minutes then pour into the cheesecloth to achieve a unique shape and to enhance the texture of the cheese. Cool completely and refrigerate.

To make the date honey:

Soak the dates (seeds removed) in the warm water up to 12 hours. Purée the dates with the honey and water until smooth, then strain through cheesecloth.

To serve, slice 8 of the figs crosswise almost completely to the bottom, but keeping the base intact. Score the remaining four figs slightly with an X on the top of each. Squeeze the fig gently from the bottom to encourage the fig to "bloom." Arrange 3 figs on each of 4 plates, place a spoonful of the cheese next to the figs, and drizzle with the date honey.

The Mostly Raw Tropical Kanten

Kanten is a vegetarian health-food version of Jell-O—perhaps the original Jell-O—and is naturally sweet without fancy sweetener replacements. It is simple and soothing, a perfect dessert to complement not complicate digestion.

⅛ cup agar flakes
1 cup apple cider or fresh apple juice
1 tablespoon arrowroot
juice of 2 medium pineapples
juice of 2 mangoes

Soak the agar flakes in ¾ cup apple cider or apple juice for half an hour while you juice the other fruits. On medium-high heat bring apple juice/agar mixture to a boil, stirring continuously. Boil for about 5 minutes. Combine arrowroot with the remaining ¼ cup apple juice or cider and add to agar mixture, return to a boil, and immediately remove from heat. Stir well, or whisk, while slowly adding pineapple and mango juices in ½-cup batches. Cool on the counter, stirring occasionally, then pour into individual bowls and refrigerate until ready to serve.

Sweet Root and Mushroom Flan with Ginger Syrup

This is another soothing custard with rich earthy notes that balance the delicate spice and sweetness. The Japanese mountain potato looks almost identical to other sweet "potatoes" (also called a yam or kumera in some places). None of these roots are related to potatoes or yams; they come from a completely different family. In any case, the Japanese mountain variety is a light gold inside, with a more subtly sweet flavor than the obvious bright-orange "sweet potato" kind. The slight difference is pleasantly familiar yet distinctly original. In this recipe, only the clear juice of the root is used. When it is combined with the rare Northwestern candy-cap mushroom, it exhibits unusual flavors that are sure to intrigue and delight your taste buds. Vegetables for dessert? Sure!

ginger syrup
- 1 cup brown rice syrup
- ½ cup maple syrup
- 2 teaspoons toasted sesame tahini
- 1 teaspoon lemon juice
- 1 tablespoon ginger juice
- 1 teaspoon vanilla extract

custard
- 2 pounds Japanese mountain potatoes
- 2 cups amazake
- 3 tablespoons agar flakes
- 1 vanilla pod, split
- 2 tablespoons candy-cap mushrooms
- ½ cup brown rice syrup
- 2 tablespoons arrowroot mixed with ½ cup rice or almond milk

½ teaspoon freshly grated nutmeg

Combine maple and brown rice syrups with tahini and whisk until smooth. Heat in a small saucepan over medium heat until bubbly. Add lemon juice and continue to simmer for 5 minutes. Add ginger juice and continue to simmer 3 more minutes. Remove from heat and add vanilla and salt. Pour into six small cups or ramekins and set aside.

To prepare the custard, first cut the mountain potato into slender spears. With the help of a vegetable juicer, juice the potato and set aside for about 15 minutes. Gently pour off the top liquid of the mountain potato juice into a saucepan. Be careful not to use any of the white starchy liquid from the bottom. Add the amazake, agar, vanilla pod, and the mushrooms. While stirring, bring to a simmer. Continue to stir and simmer for 15 minutes. Add brown rice syrup and arrowroot mixture. Return to a simmer and remove from heat immediately. Remove vanilla pod and mushrooms and cool slightly on the counter. When the custard is lightly set, whisk and divide amongst the six ramekins. Cool in refrigerator.

To serve, sprinkle nutmeg directly onto a plate, place the ramekins in a shallow pan of warm water to loosen the caramel on the bottom, and invert the ramekin onto the nutmeg. Alternatively, sprinkle the nutmeg on top of each custard and serve still in the ramekin.

The Cake

For some, birthdays are incomplete without cake and ice cream. This recipe is a joyful exploration of what cake can be even when avoiding wheat, gluten, dairy, and sugar.

    ½ cup brown rice flour
    1 cup sweet white rice flour
    ½ cup arrowroot powder
    ½ cup carob powder or cocoa powder
    ½ teaspoon salt
    2 teaspoons baking soda
    ¾ cup almond milk
    ½ cup amazake
    ½ cup coconut oil, warmed and liquefied
    2 teaspoons rice vinegar
    2 teaspoons vanilla extract
    ½ teaspoon stevia
    2 teaspoons agar powder

Combine the flours, salt, and baking soda and set aside. In a blender, combine all of the wet ingredients, the stevia, and agar. Pour the wet into the dry and mix until smooth and evenly combined. Pour into a parchment-lined 8-inch cake pan and bake for 30 minutes or until the middle of the cake springs back when touched. Remove from pan right away and cool on wire racks. When cool enough to handle, remove parchment by inverting onto another wire rack and peeling off the parchment so the cake can cool completely.

Thick and Creamy Icing

> 1 cup amazake
>
> 1 cup almond or rice milk
>
> 2 tablespoons agar flakes
>
> ¼ cup maple syrup
>
> ½ cup brown rice syrup
>
> 1 teaspoon stevia
>
> 1 tablespoon arrowroot mixed with ¼ cup rice milk
>
> ¼ cup cocoa butter *or* ¼ cup roasted tahini for vanilla icing *or* for chocolate or carob icing, ¼ cup chopped unsweetened dark chocolate or ¼ cup roasted tahini mixed with 2 tablespoons carob powder
>
> 2 tablespoons coconut oil, warmed and liquefied
>
> 1 teaspoon vanilla extract

In a medium saucepan combine amazake, almond or rice milk, and agar over medium-high heat until simmering. Stir constantly and simmer for 8 minutes. Add maple and brown rice syrups. Return to a simmer.

Stir the stevia into the arrowroot mixture and add to agar mixture, stirring well while combining; return to a simmer and remove from heat. Add cocoa butter (or chocolate or tahini), coconut oil, and vanilla. Stir until evenly combined. Pour into a shallow pan to promote rapid and even cooling, and stir occasionally until set. When the mixture is set, stir again and transfer to a bowl. Cover and refrigerate until ready to use.

Ice Creams and Sorbets

Basic Ice Cream

Most store-bought ice creams have sea vegetables in them, as carrageen is often used to replace the raw eggs that traditional ice cream recipes once included. Both agar and carrageen options are given here, and I recommend that you try both.

>   1 quart non-dairy milk
>   ½ cup maple syrup
>   ½ cup brown rice syrup
>   1 cup pineapple juice
>   2 tablespoons agar *or* ⅛ cup carrageen
>
>   1 tablespoon arrowroot mixed with 2 tablespoons rice, quinoa,
>   amaranth, hemp, or nut milk (see pages 123–124)
>   pinch of salt

Blood Orange and Vanilla Cream

>   Basic Ice Cream (see above)
>   1 vanilla pod, split lengthwise
>   1 cup blood orange juice
>   peel of 1 blood orange
>   1 tablespoon blood orange fine zest
>   ½ teaspoon stevia

Simmer ingredients (except orange zest and arrowroot mixture; see Basic Ice Cream in regard to the latter) in a saucepan until the agar or carrageen is dissolved (about 10 minutes), stirring constantly. Remove the vanilla pod, and scrape out the seeds into the pot. Add the arrowroot mixture, whisking continuously until dissolved. Remove the peel of the blood orange and add the zest. Remove from heat, add pinch of salt, and let cool, stirring or whisking occasionally.

When the mixture is cooled, refrigerate until cold then transfer to an ice cream maker or put in a shallow pan in the freezer until frozen. Remove from the freezer, stir, then return. Repeat three times to encourage a smooth consistency, then transfer to a freezer-safe container with a lid. Remove from freezer 10 minutes before serving.

Maple Toffee with Black Cumin

> Basic Ice Cream
> 1 cup non-dairy milk
> 1/4 cup toasted black cumin seeds
> 1/2 cup maple syrup
> 1 cup Suzanne's maple brown rice nectar (see Sources)
>   or brown rice syrup
> 3 tablespoons roasted sesame tahini

Simmer all of the base ingredients (except the arrowroot mixture of the base) and the additional 1 cup of non-dairy milk from this recipe in a saucepan until the agar is dissolved (about 10 minutes). Add the arrowroot slurry, whisking constantly until dissolved (2 or 3 minutes). Remove from heat, add salt, and let cool on a counter, whisking occasionally.

Cool completely in a refrigerator, then transfer to an ice cream maker or to a freezer-safe shallow pan and freeze for two hours or until nearly frozen. While the ice cream is freezing, toast the cumin seeds in a cast-iron skillet until aromatic. Add the maple syrup and brown rice nectar and stir continuously over medium-high heat for about 10 minutes. Add the tahini and remove from heat. Continue to stir. Pour into the nearly frozen ice cream. Fold in gently; do not mix in completely. Continue the freezing process and remove 20 minutes before serving.

Mocha Marshmallow Swirl

> 1 quart non-dairy milk
> 1/2 cup maple syrup
> 1/2 cup brown rice syrup
> 2 tablespoons agar *or* 1/8 cup carrageen

1 cup amazake
2 tablespoons roasted almond butter
1 cup strong roasted chicory or dandelion tea
2 tablespoons ground cacao nibs (optional—see Sources)
1 tablespoon arrowroot mixed with 2 tablespoons non-dairy milk
pinch of salt
1 teaspoon vanilla extract
1 cup Vegan Marshmallows recipe (see page 94), still warm
    and semi liquid, or cut into small pieces

Note: Omit pineapple juice in Basic Ice Cream recipe.

Combine milk, syrups, agar, amazake, almond butter, tea, and cacao nibs (if using) in a saucepan. Whisk to incorporate all ingredients. Bring to a simmer on medium heat. Cook about 10 minutes, stirring constantly, until the sea vegetables are fully dissolved. Add the arrowroot mixture, continuing to stir as the liquid returns to a simmer. Whisk in salt and vanilla extract and remove from heat. Cool and freeze as described in the above recipes. Add the marshmallow cream when the ice cream is nearly frozen. Fold in gently, not mixing in completely. Freeze according to above directions.

Coconut Ice Cream

1 quart minus $\frac{1}{2}$ cup non-dairy milk
$\frac{1}{2}$ cup maple syrup
$\frac{1}{2}$ cup brown rice syrup
$\frac{1}{2}$ cup pineapple or apple juice
2 tablespoons agar or $\frac{1}{8}$ cup carrageen
1 bruised vanilla pod, split lengthwise
2 cups coconut milk
1 tablespoon arrowroot powder mixed with 2 tablespoons
    non-dairy milk
$\frac{1}{4}$ cup candied ginger (optional)

Simmer non-dairy milk, syrups, juice, agar, and vanilla over medium-high heat, stirring constantly for 10 minutes. Remove the vanilla pod and scrape the seeds into the coconut milk. Set aside. Add the arrowroot mixture to the saucepan and whisk until fully incorporated (about 3 minutes). Add the coconut milk and salt. Return to a slow simmer then remove from heat. Cool and freeze according to above directions. If using the optional candied ginger, line a loaf pan with parchment paper once the coconut mixture is semi-frozen. Scatter ginger on the parchment paper, then spoon in semi-frozen coconut ice cream. Cover and freeze. When ready to serve, remove pan from freezer a half hour before serving. Invert onto a tray, remove the parchment, and cut the loaf into slices to serve.

Sorbet Base

Sorbet is a fresh treat in the summer. Icy-crisp flavors that are refreshing and satisfying have a great way of showcasing the fruits, berries, and herbs of the season. Use this recipe as a base for additional flavors like the recipes below.

> 2½ cups juice
> (apple cider, fresh apple juice, fresh juiced pineapple,
> or a combination of the three)
> 1 cup brown rice syrup
> ¼ cup maple syrup
> ½ teaspoon stevia
> ¼ cup arrowroot (mixed with ½ cup non-dairy milk)
> 1½ tablespoons agar flakes
> pinch of sea salt

Key Lime Sorbet Slice with Pink Peppercorn Crust

> Sorbet Base ingredients
> ¼ cup pink peppercorns
> 1 tablespoon dried rose petals
> ¼ cup dehydrated raspberries
> 1 cup fresh Key lime juice

> 1 bruised vanilla pod
> 1 tablespoon lime zest
> 1 tablespoon lemon zest
> ⅛ teaspoon liquid chlorophyll (optional)

Combine the peppercorns, rose petals, and raspberries in a spice grinder and pulse until coarsely ground. Set aside.

Combine juices, vanilla, and agar in a pot and bring to a simmer, stirring constantly until the agar is dissolved (about 10 minutes). Remove vanilla pod, scrape the seeds, and return them to the pot. Add rice syrup, maple syrup, and stevia. Return to a slight simmer and add arrowroot mixture, stirring constantly. Stir for 3 minutes, or until the mixture is no longer cloudy. Remove from heat and add the salt, zest, and chlorophyll (if using). Let cool, stirring occasionally.

When cooled completely, transfer to an ice cream maker or to a shallow pan, and freeze to the soft-set stage. Line a sheet pan with parchment paper, sprinkle the peppercorn mixture on the paper, then pour the soft-set sorbet on top of the peppercorn "crust." Return to the freezer for an hour.

Transfer the sorbet to a bread pan by picking up the parchment paper and placing in the pan. Cover with another layer of the peppercorn crust and another piece of parchment and return to the freezer. Freeze until solid.

Remove from the freezer 10 minutes before serving. Invert the pan on a cutting board, remove the outer layer of parchment, and cut with a warm knife.

Honey and Lemon Thyme Sorbet

> Sorbet Base ingredients
> ¼ cup lemon juice
> ½ cup hot water
> ½ cup fresh lemon thyme, or 2 tablespoons dried lemon thyme
> ¼ cup raw honey
> 2 tablespoons chopped fresh lemon thyme
>   (in addition to the above)

Steep the thyme in the ½ cup hot water for 20 minutes, pressing leaves occasionally to encourage a steep brew. Dissolve the agar in juice per the previous recipe. Strain the lemon thyme brew and add to the agar mixture. Stir in the stevia and the maple and rice syrups, and bring to a simmer. Add the arrowroot mixture and stir until translucent. Add lemon juice and bring temperature up to steaming. Remove from heat. Add salt and stir in the honey and the fresh lemon thyme. Cool and freeze according to the previous recipe. Each time the sorbet is set, stir to encourage a smooth texture, and transfer to a container that can be covered.

Lemon Raspberry Chamomile Sorbet-sicles

These popsicles are a big win with kids. They love the way the popsicles slide out of the molds, and kids are impressed with the layers of color. Parents are happy to see calming chamomile enjoyed and gobbled up by the youngsters!

Sorbet Base ingredients
½ cup lemon juice
1 tablespoon lemon zest
¼ cup strong chamomile tea
½ cup fresh crushed raspberries and their juice

Dissolve agar in juice according to the instructions for Key Lime Sorbet above. Add stevia, maple, and rice syrup (of the Sorbet Base) and bring to a simmer again. Add arrowroot mixture and stir constantly for 3 minutes. Remove from heat and add lemon juice.

Divide mixture among three bowls. To one add the zest, to another add chamomile tea, and to the third add raspberries. Let cool, then put in the freezer. Remove from the freezer every hour or so and stir to encourage a smooth texture. After the mixtures are nearly frozen, spoon into popsicle molds in alternating layers beginning with lemon, then chamomile, then raspberry. Return to the freezer.

seven

Salt and Heating Oil Essentials

Salt

Since the beginning of culinary exploration, salt has been used to preserve and give flavor to foods. Unfortunately, like many commodities, the salt industry has many faces. A variety of salts is available, and they range in value dramatically. I like to have a few types of salt on hand in my kitchen. I favor fine speckled mineral salts for the table, and coarse hand-harvested sea salts for cooking. There are some special salts too, however, and each chef has his or her favorite.

Fleur de Sal

Meaning "flower of the salt," this hand-harvested salt is commonly used to bring out the flavors of naturally sweet foods. Fleur de sal is the very first bits of salt that form on top of the salt beds. The crystals bloom quickly and are harvested right away. The nature of this salt is like that of spring, delicately reminding us of the sweetness underfoot. Artichokes, asparagus, chocolate, and figs are just a few foods that shine under a sprinkling of this fine salt. Best used as a finishing salt (sprinkle on the cooked foods).

Sal Gris

Sal gris is a product of concentrated salt water, as opposed to pure evaporation. Made on site, on the ocean's edge, sal gris results when salt water is collected during the high tide, allowed to evaporate during low tide, then more salt water is added again at high tide. When the salt begins to outweigh the water, the two separate, and the salt settles to the bottom. This process is what differentiates the sal gris from many other salts. It is heavy by nature, and full of sea minerals. I would not recommend it in desserts or in cases where you may want to bring out sweetness. Instead, I use it sparingly to accentuate the depth of dry-roasted autumn vegetables like winter squash, parsnips, turnips, and celery root.

Australian Pink Flakes

Salt flakes are a special treat for finishing dishes. The flakes melt evenly on the tongue and are mild in saltiness. These peach-colored flakes are harvested in an effort to de-salinate Australian basin pools. The flakes are colored by the carotene-rich algae that grow in the basin. Delicate foods are best to celebrate this salt—foods that have little or no other seasoning seem to burst with flavor when met with these crystals. Try with fresh steamed octopus or scallops, fresh crab meat, or flash-steamed baby carrots.

Himalayan Salt Crystals

This salt is what remains of the ancient sea that once filled the valley between the Himalayan mountains. It has an antique quality, like an artifact treasured and brought out to impress guests. The flavor here is full of earthy minerals, and it complements foods that share these qualities. Red meats, roasted vegetables, and slow-cooked beans all benefit from a dash of these fine pink salts.

Utah Mineral Salt

Speckled with the reds of iron, this salt is a great table salt as well as an ingredient of cooked dishes. It gently brings out the flavor in most dishes. This salt is also readily available to purchase at most co-ops and natural food stores and, therefore, a great alternative to refined sea salt.

Fine Sea Salt

There are many different varieties of salt under the heading "fine sea salt." It is hard to distinguish flavor based on origination alone. How the salt is harvested, cured, and stored is what differentiates one product from another. Do your research and select a salt that is harvested close to you, using methods that you are in alliance with. See the Sources list for contact information.

Smoked Sea Salt

When adding creativity to a dish, smoked salt is a culinary delight. The salt gives an obvious smoked flavor and aroma to any food it is combined with, yet is not overpowering. Like smoked peppercorns, sea vegetables, or smoked fish, smoked salt is cured using locally available woods to give flavor to the salt. There is a large variety of flavors, and this product is available both in coarse and fine ground crystals. Check the Sources list for contact information.

Hawaiian Black Salt

Mixed with the black lava that is so abundant in Hawaii, this coarse salt brings mystery and depth to the table. The crunch of this black salt is complemented by steamed or fried beets, green beans, edamame, carrots, and other steamed vegetables. Offer this salt as a condiment to get conversation started or to initiate "diner presence"—when we want our fellow diners to be present with the meal we have presented.

Hawaiian Red Clay Salt

This coarse salt is combined with the red clay that is abundant in Hawaii. When ground in a mortar and pestle, the salt is silky smooth and colorful. Traditionally it is used to give flavor to ceremonial roasts. The color and texture of Hawaiian red clay salt invites you to do the same.

Celtic Sea Salts

Considered by some as the most "healthful" salt, these salts are low in sodium. They are often still moist when purchased. I prefer to lightly crush the granules and add at the end of cooking. Lentils, baked figs, and wild game delight under the influence of this hand-crafted, Old World salt.

Heating Oils

Some oils have a low heating point and are not the best to cook with. The oils that I recommend for safe heating are discussed below. Depending on your personal dietary requirements, the oil that you cook with may vary from season to season, or according to what is available to you.

Coconut Oil

In many parts of the world this is the primary oil used for cooking. I prefer to use this as my cooking oil when I am deep-frying or making tempura, cooking in the tropics, avoiding animal products, or if what I am cooking is sweet. Organic coconut oil is easy to find and not particularly expensive. It does not go rancid at high temperatures and will last a very long time if stored properly in a dry, cool, and dark environment. See the Sources list.

Ghee

Clarified butter or ghee is used throughout Indonesia and India. Once the butter has been clarified it is a stable fat; the moisture and sugars have been removed so, unlike butter, it will not burn at high temperatures. Ghee can be used in baking mixtures and as a frying oil, or to oil a baking tray.

Purchase butter from a local farmer and make your own ghee by gently melting the butter on low heat in a saucepan. When foam appears, gently skim off. Continue to heat on low for 10 minutes and remove from heat. As the butter cools, it will separate into two masses, a heavy whitish milky mass on the bottom, and a lighter oily clearish mass floating on top. You want to keep this liquid on top. When the butter is cool enough to handle but not completely cooled (it will harden), gently pour the top half of the liquid into a container, being careful not to combine the two layers. Discard the milky bottom layer and store the ghee in an airtight container.

Animal Fat

Animal fat or lard has been used since the beginning of time as a cooking oil. For some, however, the thought of using animal fat goes against everything they know about healthful cooking. I completely understand this dilemma, having faced it numerous times myself. However, after spending several winters in Vermont, I have come to understand the benefits of consuming animal fat. When using animal fat, I am cautious as to how much oil I am using and how often I use it. This enables me to have an awareness about my food that I did not have before. I believe that there is a health risk if you are cooking all of your food in animal fat every day of the year. If you prepare your food in harmony with the seasons you would not have this opportunity. Use animal fat occasionally for cooking in the coldest months to quickly sear or broil mochi, meat, or vegetables. Duck and bacon fat are the easiest to render.

eight

Special Preparations

Nuts, Seeds, Grains, and Beans

Prepared Pumpkin Seeds, Cashews, Almonds, Macadamias, Pecans, Walnuts, Pine Nuts, and Sunflower Seeds

Soak seeds in warm, salted water all day or overnight. Drain and scatter evenly on a baking sheet. Dry the seeds or nuts in a warm oven (180–200°F) for at least 12 hours, or until crisp and dry. Store in an airtight container.

Almond Milk and Almond Paste

Soak the almonds as described above, and rinse after 12 hours. Process the almonds in food processor or with an immersion blender until they resemble a smooth paste. Add a bit of water if needed. Combine the paste with an equal amount of water and cover tightly. Leave the mixture at room temperature for 12 hours, then strain. Reserve both the liquid and the solids. To strain, use a cheesecloth, cover the mouth of the jar containing the almond paste, and invert over a wider container, capturing the "milk." Squeeze the remaining "milk" from the almond paste reserved in the cheesecloth. Store the milk in the refrigerator and use the almond paste for other recipes, or dehydrate on a baking sheet in a 150° oven for 4 hours or until it resembles a fine almond flour. Store in an airtight container.

Sesame and Hemp Seeds

Soak seeds at room temperature overnight. Use a clear glass jar, uncovered. Drain seeds by covering mouth of jar with cheesecloth and simply pouring off the water. Rinse the seeds several times and place the jar on its side (cheesecloth still attached) in a warm dark cabinet. Rinse the seeds three or four times a day for 2–3 days.

The tiny sprouts can be stored in the refrigerator or dehydrated on a baking sheet in a warm oven (150°F) for 2–5 hours then ground and stored in an airtight container.

Rice, Quinoa, Amaranth, and Lentils

Cover in water and soak with juice of half a lemon for at least 12 hours. Rinse after 12 hours and continue soaking up to 48 hours. Drain and cook in equal amounts of water, but add more water as needed (the more water the grain takes in, the plumper and more succulent the texture) or, in warmer temperatures, steam in a rice steamer or a steamer lined with cheesecloth until cooked through.

Rice, Quinoa, or Amaranth Milk

Soak the grains as described above, 3 parts water to 1 part grain. Cook the grain 3–6 hours, on low heat, adding more water as needed. The grain should be well cooked and very soft. Process the grain in a blender or food processor with enough water to fully liquefy the grain. Store in an airtight container for 12 hours. Strain, using several layers of cheesecloth, and store in the refrigerator.

Beans of All Sorts

Wash well and remove any stones or broken beans, and cover in cold water and juice from half a lemon. Soak 12 hours, rinse, and cover again with water and juice of half a lemon. Continue rinsing and soaking the beans for a total of up to 36 hours.

To cook the beans, cover completely with an ample amount of water. Simmer the beans in a large pot or crockpot with 2–4 strips of kombu or local kelp for at least 2 hours. (If using a slow cooker or crockpot, you will need to let the beans cook 12–24 hours.)

Light Broths

Dashi

Dashi is a basic broth used in most Japanese soups and sauces. Variations may include soy sauce, tamari, bonito, or other dried fish. Kombu has been used for centuries as a basic broth—it adds flavor as well as provides a variety of healing qualities.

>4 sticks of kombu (3 inches long)
>10 cups water

Place the kombu in a pot with the water and bring to a boil. Lower heat and simmer for 2 hours. Slightly cool, and remove kombu before serving.

Fish Broth

>bones and heads of 3–6 wild-harvested fish
>½ bunch celery, leaves included
>2 carrots, coarsely chopped
>3 inches fresh ginger, sliced
>3 cloves garlic, peeled and sliced
>½ teaspoon peppercorns
>¼ cup apple cider vinegar or rice wine vinegar

Place the ingredients in a large pot or crockpot and cover with water. Bring to a simmer, cover, and cook for 6 to 24 hours, occasionally removing any foam that has risen to the surface. Strain, cool, and refrigerate or freeze until ready to use.

Chicken, Duck, or Turkey Broth

>3 pounds chicken, duck, or turkey pieces with bones
>1 onion, sliced
>3 cloves garlic, sliced
>½ bunch celery, with leaves
>3 carrots, coarsely chopped
>2 tablespoons apple cider vinegar or rice vinegar

1 lemon, seeds removed
1 bunch parsley, cilantro, or nettles

Place all ingredients in a large pot or crockpot and cover completely, with an additional few inches, in cold water. Bring to a simmer, cover, and let cook 2–4 hours (remove any foam that rises to the surface). With a pair of tongs, remove the large bones and let cool in a colander. When cool enough to touch, break the bones in half and return to the pot. Continue to simmer an additional 4–20 hours, occasionally skimming off any foam that sits on the surface. Strain the broth and store in the refrigerator or freezer. Separate the vegetables and meat from the bones and skin and reserve for another use.

Light Vegetable Broth

3 onions, peeled and sliced
1 head celery, leaves attached
3 carrots, coarsely chopped
6 cloves garlic, peeled and sliced
2 yellow beets, sliced in half
2 parsnips, sliced in half
1 medium-sized sweet potato, sliced in quarters
1 head broccoli, chopped
1 bunch kale
1 strip wakame
1 cup peas
1 bunch parsley, nettles, or cilantro

Combine all ingredients except the peas and parsley (or nettles or cilantro) in a large pot or crockpot and cover with an ample amount of water. On medium heat bring to a simmer and cook, covered, 6–24 hours. Add the peas and parsley to the pot 10 minutes before removing from the heat. With an immersion blender, blend the stock until all the ingredients are in tiny bits. Strain through a single layer of cheesecloth and refrigerate or freeze.

Dark Broths

Roasted Chicken, Duck, or Turkey Broth

> at least 3 pounds of bones or 3 pounds chicken, duck,
>   or turkey pieces
> salt
> freshly ground pepper
> 3 tablespoons dried nettles, savory, lemon thyme, lemon balm,
>   and/or sage
> 2 heads garlic, one end cut off, head still intact
> 2 onions, cut in half
> 3 carrots, cut in half
> 2 tablespoons ghee (see page 118)
> 2 lemons, oranges, apples, pears, or seasonal tree fruit, cut in half
> 2 tablespoons apple cider vinegar

To roast:

Place all ingredients, except the fruit and vinegar, into a shallow roasting pan. (If you are using raw meat, rub with ghee, salt, and pepper, and push the herbs under the skin before putting in the pan.) Roast in a hot oven (375°F) for 1 hour, basting the vegetables and meat as needed. Remove from the oven, allowing the dish to cool enough to handle the bones and/or meat. Chop the bones in half, revealing the marrow within, and place them with the rest of the roasted ingredients into a pot or crockpot with the tree fruits and vinegar. Fill with water and bring to a simmer. Cover and cook 6–24 hours, skimming any foam that you find on the surface. Strain before storing in the refrigerator or freezer.

Roasted Vegetable Broth

> Use ingredients for Light Vegetable Broth (see page 126).

Roast all the ingredients (except the wakame, kale, peas, or parsley) in a 350° oven for 1 hour. Combine the ingredients in a large pot or crockpot and continue as described for Light Vegetable Broth.

Kombu Mushroom Broth

      6 cups mixed fresh mushrooms, sliced

      2 cups dried shiitake or wild mushrooms, covered in water
          and soaked for at least 4 hours

      6 strips of kombu or wakame

      ½ cup wheat-free tamari or Bragg Liquid Aminos

      1 onion, peeled and sliced

      5 cloves garlic, peeled and sliced

      2 tablespoons sesame oil

Roast the fresh mushrooms in a hot oven (425°F) for 15 minutes, or until shriveled-looking (but not charred!). Combine all ingredients (except the sesame oil), including the shiitake soaking water, in a large pot or crockpot. Cover completely with water, plus an additional 2 inches. Bring to a simmer, cover, and cook on low heat 4–12 hours. Strain, add sesame oil, and store in the refrigerator. Reserve the shiitakes and kombu for another use.

Beef, Venison, or Lamb Broth

      1 large or 2–3 smaller beef or lamb bones with the marrow

      1–3 pounds beef or lamb for stewing—on the bone if you can find it

      2 onions, peeled and sliced

      3 carrots, sliced

      1 head celery, roughly chopped

      1 head garlic, peeled and sliced

      ½ tablespoon peppercorns

      3 inches ginger, thyme, savory, or sage

      1 lemon, orange, mandarin, or seasonal citrus, sliced in half
          and seeds removed

      3 tablespoons salt

      ½ cup apple cider vinegar or rice vinegar

Before making this broth, you can roast all of the ingredients (except the vinegar), plus any other vegetable you have around, in a hot (350°) oven for about 30 to 45 minutes. This is not essential, but roasting does give depth to the flavor of the bones. However, should you choose not to, that is fine too; this is a hearty broth and can even be enjoyed as a stew first, then strained for later use as a broth.

Combine all of the ingredients in a large pot or crockpot, cover with an abundance of water, and simmer on low heat, covered, for at least 6 hours and up to 36. Skim off any foam you see settling on the surface. Strain, making sure that all of the marrow has escaped the bone, and reserve any meat you may want for further uses. Refrigerate or freeze the broth.

nine

Sources

Let's face it, the world was discovered, slaves traded, and colonies settled in pursuit of exotic spices, essential oils, grains, salt, sugar, and seeds. As the politics of genetically modified foods and the economics of oil and free trade wreak havoc throughout all countries, the price for food can no longer be tracked. This reality is often depressing and hard to accept. In response to these issues, I encourage you to feed your family at least one local meal a week. Turn Thanksgiving or New Year's dinner into a totally local organic one, sourcing or growing as much as you can for at least that one meal a year. Attend your local farmers market, and ask your local food store to carry and label local foods. Look for fair-trade commodities, and cultivate a relationship with at least one food producer. Be proud of your efforts—your consumer power is the energy that keeps businesses in business. Be involved in your own food production and enjoy being nourished by your community.

Local Food Networks

Australia

The Organics Directory
The Organics Directory is a colorful look into the Australian organic industry. Includes photos of farmers and food producers as well as contact information for all kinds of organic food-related businesses, including farms.
www.theorganicsdirectory.com.au

Canada and USA

Biodynamic Farming and Gardening Association Inc.
This association has a website that offers contact information for establishing a CSA (Community-Supported Agriculture) enterprise anywhere in North America. The site also has useful links and

information regarding biodynamic agriculture.
www.biodynamics.com
Telephone: 888-516-7797

Buy Local Food Movement

This organization was founded by Guillermo Payet to help identify, support, and create an organic food network within the United States. Their website offers collaborative links to local food organizations throughout the United States, with details including contact information for farmers, CSAs, markets, co-ops, and restaurants in each state. This site is very easy to use and an inspiring resource for consumers. I highly recommend it to anyone looking to know more about their local (USA) food web.
www.localharvest.org

Canadian Organic Growers

National information network for organic farmers, consumers, and markets. This site includes links to numerous directories and calendars throughout Canada.
www.cog.ca

Equiterre

Canadian CSA and fair-trade network with extensive links and information.
www.equiterre.org

Sustainable Table

Search for stores, farms, restaurants, and organizations within Canadian and United States foodsheds.
www.eatwellguide.org

wildfoods

"Wildman" Steve Brills is a foraging guide who has created his own niche in New York City. Steve offers city dwellers the opportunity to become more educated in the abundance within the city through classes, workshops, literature, and walks through the park.
www.wildmanstevebrill.com

Europe

The Open Garden Foundation

Serving Hungary with organic food boxes and CSAs, through collective efforts of local food producers, as well as information and links for organic farms, shops, and markets in Hungary.
www.nyitottkert.hu

Biobank Italy

Biobank is like a phone book for organic businesses. With over 5,000 contacts, it is one of the most thorough collections in Europe. To purchase the book or to learn more about the project, contact www.biobank.it

allesBio

allesBio has more than 4,000 entries for direct sellers of organic products within Germany.
www.allesbio.de
www.organic-europe.net
Search the address database to contact a farmer near you.

United Kingdom

Local Food Works

This organization has links and information for farms in the UK.
www.localfoodworks.org

National Association of Farmers Markets

This association's website is very easy to navigate and offers schedules for farmers markets in the UK.
www.farmersmarkets.net

whyorganic.org

This web-based organization offers a directory of organic farms, markets, restaurants, and butchers throughout the UK. Also includes information about box schemes (CSAs).
www.whyorganic.org

South Africa

go-organic.com
This site has a directory of farmers, markets, and wholesalers in South Africa.
www.go-organic.co.za

New Zealand

Organic Pathways
Check out their website for a full directory of organic farms and businesses throughout New Zealand.
www.organicpathways.co.nz

International Organizations

World Links
Links to organic organizations around the world.
www.ifoam.org

Green Trade
A directory of more than 2,000 sellers of certified organic products. This website is a great place to source many of your pantry ingredients.
www.greentrade.net

Fair Trade Federation
A website provides links and contact information for markets carrying products with their certification, along with great information and photos of the food producers.
www.fairtradefederation.org

Fair Trade
This interesting site has information about farmers as well as where to purchase their products. The organization carries fair-trade rice, spices, and nuts as well as fruit, chocolate, and tea.
www.fairtrade.org.uk

Transfair
This organization carries chocolate and fresh fruit as well as coffee.
www.transfairusa.org

Willing Workers on Organic Farms
This organization is dedicated to helping travelers gain experience working on organic farms and enjoying economical adventures through networking with organic farmers and businesses around the globe. The best way to travel, in my opinion!
www.wwoof.org

Additional Sources

Chocolate

Cocoa Camino
La Siembra Co-op works with fair-trade certified co-op producers and sells fair-trade cane sugar as well as cocoa products including chocolate. Photos of the farmers and information about their company are easily accessible through the website.
www.lasiembra.coop/cn

Sweet Earth
Sellers of fair-trade organic chocolate grown by co-ops in the Dominican Republic and Costa Rica.
www.sweetearthchocolates.com

Fair Trade
This great site has information about farmers as well as where to purchase their products: fair trade rice, spices, and nuts as well as fruit, chocolate, and tea.
www.fairtrade.org.uk

Transfair
This organization carries chocolate and fresh fruit as well as coffee.
www.transfairusa.org

Coconut Oil

Coconut Research Center

Resources include links to organic, fair-trade coconut oil distributors all around the world.

www.coconutresearchcenter.org

Gluten-free Pantry Items

Amazake and Mochi

Since 1979, Grainaissance has been dedicated to making brown rice products. The company now sells amazake and mochi through most natural food stores. For nutritional information, purchasing locations, and recipes, check out their website.

www.grainaissance.com

Brown Rice Pasta

My favorite gluten-free organic pasta in a variety of shapes is available via the following link:

www.tinkyada.com

Brown Rice Syrup and Agave Nectar

Organic gluten-free alternative sweeteners including maple nectar (maple-infused brown rice syrup) and agave syrup:

www.suzannes-specialties.com

Rice and Rice Flour

This website is shared by Lotus Foods, distributors of fine heirloom rice varieties. Products include heirloom rice as well as rare rice flours.

www.worldpantry.com

Tamari and Miso

Tamari and miso products as well as my favorite black sesame crackers are available from the following manufacturer's link:

www.san-j.com

Vegan Marshmallows

www.veganstore.com

Mushrooms

Links to mushroom growers' resources and mushroom kits:
www.mushrooms.com

Salt and Pepper

Big Tree Bali

Big Tree Farm produces artisan salt, specialty pepper, coconut
sugar, and other spices and is dedicated to small-scale sustainable
farming and ecotourism.
www.bigtreebali.com

Hawaii Kai Company

Sellers of Palm Island Gourmet salts, including Black Lava and Red
Clay Salts.
www.hawaiikaico.com

Khoisan Trading Company

South African hand-harvested salt products. Their product range
includes a sea vegetable salt.
www.khoisantrading.co.za

Maine Sea Salt Company

Makers of solar-evaporated and smoked salts, including Atlantic
smoked salt.
www.maineseasalt.com

Pepper Passion

Sellers of fine salts and peppercorns.
www.pepper-passion.com

Salt Traders

A Web-based business that sells and describes more than 20 varieties of salt. Most salts are sourced.
www.salttraders.com

Saltworks

Online shopping for fine salts.
www.saltworks.us

Sea Vegetables

Dolphin Sea Vegetable Company
Belfast, North Ireland
www.dolphinseaveg.com

Emerald Cove Seaweed Products
Asian sea vegetables and nori sheets.
www.great-eastern-sun.com

Island Herbs and BC Kelp
British Columbia, Canada. Visit this website for information and
products, including sea vegetables.
www.ryandrum.com

Ironbound Island
Winter Harbor, Maine. Sustainable sea vegetable harvesters.
www.ironboundisland.com

King Island Produce
Tasmania, Australia. Harvesters Peta and Dennis collect and sell
kelp and other added-value products, including an assortment of
kelp pickles and other condiments.
www.kip.com.au

Maine Coast Sea Vegetables
Franklin, Maine. One of the oldest sea vegetable companies in the
United States.
www.seaveg.com

Mendocino Sea Vegetable Company
Philo, California.
www.seaweed.net

Naturespirit Herbs
Williams, Oregon. This website has a wealth of detailed information regarding folklore, descriptions, and medicinal information
for sea vegetables. To place an order, call 541-846-7995, or use the
website.
www.naturespiritherbs.com

Ocean Harvest Sea Vegetable Co.
Northern California
www.ohsv.net

Ocean Herbs
Israel. Offers a variety of sea vegetable seasoning mixes.
www.oceanherbs.com

Outer Coast Seaweed Company
Sooke, British Columbia, Canada
www.outercoastseaweeds.com

Pacific Harvest
New Zealand's primary sea vegetable company, specializing in karengo and other native sea vegetables.
www.pacificharvest.co.nz

Pacific Sun Sea Vegetables
Ucluet, British Columbia, Canada
www.kelp.ca

Pacific Wildcraft
A family-oriented wild foods company located in Mendocino, California. To place an order, call 707-357-0375 or send an email to info@pacificwildcraft.com.
www.pacificwildcraft.com

Quality Sea Veg
Cloughglass, County Donegal, Ireland
Maire Devlin's sea vegetable company.
www.seaveg.co.uk

Rising Tide Sea Vegetables
Mendocino, California, specializing in sea palm and other native varieties.
www.loveseaweed.com

Roland's Sea Vegetables
Grand Manan, New Brunswick, Canada
www.rolandsdulse.com

Sea Breeze
Mendocino, California
moonmaid@mcn.org

Seagreens
West Sussex, United Kingdom and Norway
www.seagreens.com

Spices

Forestrade
Distributor of organic, fair-trade spices and coffee. Their website is full of information, photos, and news about developing co-operatives, growers, and new markets.
www.forestrade.com

Nirmala's Kitchen
Online supplier of sourced exotic and heirloom spices and salts.
www.nirmalaskitchen.com

Wholespice Company
Organic herbs and spices as well as organic arrowroot powder. Spices are ground to order. Located in California.
www.wholespice.com

Vanilla

Facts, products, links, and legends are included in this conscious website founded by Patricia Rain.
www.vanilla.com

Quinoa

Andean Naturals
Check out their site to buy quinoa direct and to see beautiful photos and information.
www.andeannaturals.com

INDEX

ABOUT THE AUTHOR

Crystal June Maderia is a cook, caterer, and consultant to people with diet-specific needs. She has been inspired by food since she was a child and continues to cultivate an intimacy with food through her work with food producers in her local community and throughout the world. Maderia has lived and traveled throughout New Zealand, Australia, and the United States, most recently having lived in Mendocino, California. She currently resides in Montpelier, Vermont, with her partner and two sons, Moses and Fela.

In late 2006, Maderia and business partner Alanna Dorf opened Kismet, a restaurant and catering service that specializes in local artisanal grains, meats, and cheeses; seasonal produce; organic, single-origin coffees, teas, and spices; gluten-free products; and handmade organic chocolates.

You can visit their website at www.kismetkitchen.com.